HISTORY
——5 to 11——

Joan Blyth

Hodder & Stoughton

A MEMBER OF THE HODDER HEADLINE GROUP

British Library Cataloguing in Publication Data

A catalogue for this title is available from the British Library

ISBN 0 340 58912 4

First published 1994
Impression number   10   9   8   7   6   5   4   3   2   1
Year   1998   1997   1996   1995   1994

Typeset by Wearset, Boldon, Tyne and Wear.
Printed in Great Britain for Hodder & Stoughton Educational, a
division of Hodder Headline Plc, 338 Euston Road, London
NW1 3BH by The Bath Press, Lower Bristol Road, Bath.

To
Roy Hughes, Chairman
and the members of the
Primary Committee
of the
Historical Association

Contents

List of illustrations

Acknowledgements

Before and after the setting up of the National Curriculum History Working Group in 1989, I was involved in discussions about the future of primary-school history. Therefore I much appreciated the invitation by Hodder and Stoughton to re-write my *History 5 to 9*, published in 1988, to make it more relevant to the new curriculum. I received sound initial advice about the shape and nature of the new version from Penelope Harnett, of the University of the West of England; from Peter Knight, of the University of Lancaster; and from Sallie Purkis, editor of the well-known Longman series *A Sense of History* and now a freelance consultant. Colleagues on the Historical Association's Primary Committee have contributed case studies from their own teaching: for this, thanks are due to Paul Bish, Russell Carter, Penelope Harnett and Linda Holdridge. In addition, Jo Lawrie, Grahame Banks and Robert Guyver have added their specialities.

Throughout the hours of thinking, correspondence, drafting, re-writing and checking, I have been supported by my husband Alan Blyth, by my word-processing secretary Lego Moody and above all, by my editor, Elizabeth Wright.

This book is a tribute to many friends. I hope that it will also be useful to many teachers.

The publishers and I would like to acknowledge the following individuals and organisations for allowing me to reproduce photographic materials: The Shakespeare Birthplace Trust for the cover picture: *A Family Saying Grace before the Meal* by Anthonius Claeissins (c1538–1613) on display at Hall's Croft, Stratford-upon-Avon; The British Library for permission to reproduce *David playing a harp* – a painting made at Canterbury at King Offa's request; The Victoria and Albert Museum for the picture, *Unknown Young Man*, by Nicholas Hilliard, reproduced by courtesy of the Board of Trustees of the Victoria and Albert Museum; North Yorkshire County Library for the right to reproduce *Ancient View of the town, Castle, and Harbour of Scarborough*; Edwin Smith for the picture of Sir Humphrey Chetham's Monument, *A Seventeenth-Century Schoolboy*, by W. Theed, Manchester Cathedral; the late Mrs P.A. Tritton of Parham Park, Sussex for the right to reproduce *Queen Victoria*, by William Fowler; The Illustrated London News Picture Library for *The Cotton Famine: a group of Mill Operatives at Manchester*; The Science Museum for the right to reproduce 'First Class Railway Carriage' (Model); The National Trust Photographic Library and Geoffrey Frosh for the right to reproduce the 'The front room of Mr Straw's House', photographed by Geoffrey Frosh; The Public Record Office for the right to reproduce the poster 'Save fuel for Battle'; *the Guardian*, and Alan Reevell, for the right to reproduce the photograph of the prefabricated house; English Heritage for the right to reproduce the photograph of the Medieval Merchant's House, Southampton; the Welsh National Curriculum for the diagrams used in Figures 2 and 3; and the Devon Local Education Authority for the diagram in Figure 21. Special thanks to the teachers and pupils of Highfield Primary School, Urmston, Manchester for Figures, 17, 18 and 19 and to Paul Noble for Figures 23, 24, 25 and 26. Finally thanks to Corsley Church of England Primary School, Warminster for Figure 27.

Introduction

The National Curriculum for history in primary schools has rendered pre-1991 publications out of date from the standpoint of content. Thus this book replaces *History 5 to 9* (published by Hodder and Stoughton in 1988) and extends the age range to 11.

Part I sets primary history in its educational context and shows how recent research can help the classroom teacher. Part II is based on the Attainment Target and Programmes of Study in the 1994 Dearing Proposals. This revision, whilst reducing the amount of compulsory content, also encourages teachers to develop historical understanding through other subjects, through information technology, and through the use they make of time freed from the prescribed programmes of study. Part III returns to more general considerations, using case-studies by practising teachers to show how their preparation and practice have recently been adapted to the National Curriculum.

The whole book attempts to help teachers to select essential elements of the study units in a way which allows them to avoid becoming too over-burdened with preparation.

I hope that most of the illustrations will be sought from the references and used by teachers in their classrooms.

PART I

Primary children and history

History and children's need for the past

History is all that ever happened in the world, the record of whatever happened (the narrative or story) and the interpretation or explanation of that record at the time, and since. Aspects of history include time, story/narrative, artefacts, environment and eventually a world framework. But history is essentially about adults and their actions. Teachers play a very important part in children's understanding because, as adults, they can try to interpret the thoughts and actions of adults. This requires knowledge about the past and help in interpreting it from their own reading and attendance at in-service courses. I believe that children *need* the past, and teachers should be helped to show them how it can be used and built upon for the future.

Too many teachers have unhappy experiences of history from their own secondary school days unless they had encyclopaedic memories or were fortunate enough to encounter the rare inspired teacher of history. Many, therefore, have little impetus to seek out interesting ways of approaching the subject with young children. They have a traditional view of history as being the chronology of all countries of the world in all classes of society, perhaps with an emphasis on 'kings and things' prominent in publishers' catalogues, but complex and remote from ordinary peoples' lives. But family history, oral history and local history are as valid a form of history as the more traditional approaches of kings, wars and politics. They should remember in the words of the archaeologist Dr C. Hills, that 'the past is not another place'.

Having decided that he/she is capable of understanding this area of teaching, the general primary teacher must consider why children *need* the past in order to make his/her efforts worthwhile and tailor them to the children's requirements. There seem to be three areas to bear in mind. The first is the personal, inward-looking need to help the child to develop as a well-adjusted stable adult. Another is the area concerned with other people, the outward-looking needs of the child in relation to society. The third area embraces the practical needs of the child using the essential historical concepts and skills learnt in a study of the past. A sense of historic time is the greatest contribution history can make to all other areas of learning.

HISTORY FULFILS THE INWARD-LOOKING NEEDS OF CHILDREN

Human nature makes mankind naturally self-centred and therefore selfish. The education of children at home and at school is part of the process of leading children from this inward-looking preoccupation to thinking of others and being unselfish in attitudes, words and actions. Knowing about themselves, their families and their past helps children to understand why they are as they are, for good or ill. According to Arthur Marwick, history is man's collective memory which he loses at his peril. 'As a man without memory and self-knowledge is a man adrift, so a society without a memory (or more correctly, without recollection) and self-knowledge would be a society adrift.' (Marwick, 1970) As a philosopher-historian has written, 'History teaches us what man has done and thus what man is' (Collingwood, 1946) and for children to know themselves, and what they can and cannot do, is the beginning of personal wisdom and a happy life. For example, Francis Drake was the sort of person who dared to circumnavigate the world in the small ship *The Golden Hind*, but most of us could not contemplate this. Both the Romans and Hitler were obsessed by power and were ambitious in their acquisition of land; they failed miserably in the end, as did Napoleon Bonaparte. The moral is to accept your strengths and limitations and plan your life within those. How human beings react to other people and events is unpredictable and uncertain both inside and outside the family. Children too often become victims of adults and the past can help them to be on their guard and also understand the whims of those around them. The recent pressure on children not to go with strangers has led to direct teaching from the past experience of society. Children have been found to be quick to learn.

Many adults lead unbalanced emotional lives on account of their upbringing and are unable to experience outgoing, empathetic feelings. John Slater's description of the response of one primary headmaster who taught his children about nineteenth-century factory children from original sources, is direct and simple. He was trying to achieve heartfelt response from them: 'I want to make them weep.' (Slater, 1978) Thus teaching about the past can begin to overcome 'the stiff upper lip' which has caused so many small boys problems in their future relationships. This sympathy can also be developed into an awareness of the overt and hidden discrimination suffered by various sections of society.

Children who understand themselves, their thoughts and weaknesses, become more confident, self-respecting people, knowing that they have a purposeful role to fulfil in society. Knowing about people in the past and discussing them with teachers and their peers helps children to have the confidence to cope with people in life. The determination of William Wilberforce to end slavery, Florence Nightingale to improve the care of the sick and Marie Curie to find a cure for cancer are examples of endurance in the cause of social betterment which can give children confidence in difficult tasks.

HISTORY FULFILS THE OUTWARD-LOOKING NEEDS OF CHILDREN

Children who understand themselves and have confidence in their powers, however limited they may be, need to move out from this position to try to understand the world around them. This includes other children, their families (near and far) and their teachers. It also includes knowledge of many areas of information for an appreciation of various forms of the media. This is particularly important for the understanding of television both at home and at school. School television programmes are usually explained by the teacher and limited in duration, but television in many homes is unexplained and ever present. Young children who are victims of this social situation need particular help from school. References to South Africa, Ireland, Somalia, Bosnia/Serbia and Maastricht are confusing to children unless they have an outline knowledge of the issues involved. Most of these issues depend upon geography but are all historically based and have a past history going back far beyond the birth of the children concerned.

Celebrations and anniversaries which fill the media encourage an awareness of the past through their very nature. Although Christmas is a religious festival, Christ's birth and life happened in time and the references to his work in the Bible depict the social life of the first century AD in a particular country. Royal weddings involve knowledge of family trees, traditions, customs and relationships far into the past. Resources for schools on these occasions are plentiful and usually well-documented. Royal weddings can be compared; those of Princess Elizabeth in 1947, the Princess Royal in 1992, Queen Victoria in 1839 and Henry VIII. (Why did Henry VIII have so many weddings?) Centenaries of schools have proved most successful whole-school activities linking five- to eleven-year-olds. Comparison of a school in 1894 with their own in 1994 is very relevant, especially if it is the same school. It is an easy way to develop the concept of change. Guy Fawkes' unsuccessful attempt to blow up Parliament is celebrated each November. Teachers of infants have wanted to explain its importance but do not know how to. What is 'Parliament'? Why should 'Catholics' want to blow it up? They do not want to do this in 1994. Parents and teachers are bound to have to face up to explanations of the two world wars and the conflict in Ireland by using the past. Children aged seven will not be put off by being told to wait until they are nine to understand it, since the media is ever present and compelling. Certain advertisers use historical characters to get over their message. Children are bombarded by advertisements from television, hoardings in streets, food packets and comics.

Another outward-looking need of young children is for them to develop an interest in people and to learn to tolerate the points of view of others. The past is concerned with interaction of people and events all over the world. If a young child can begin a life-long interest in Roman remains, Native American Indians or Mogul emperors, to give only a few examples, he/she will always have a leisure interest and be a frequenter of libraries.

Young children have a passion for specific facts which build up personal identity. John West has proved that six-year-olds have more patience and determination to work out a tricky piece of palaeography (old handwriting) than older children. Their learning of the alphabet and how to read is so near to them that this is only another challenge to be pursued regardless of time pressure. This can also lead to an interest in other alphabets, such as Egyptian hieroglyphics. It can also be of value in multicultural education, learning a foreign language and even the invention of their own alphabet.

Interest in the past is often fired by one imaginative experience or story, whether told by the teacher, seen on a television programme, or read in a story book. The good story has a great influence on children and adults. There are many exciting real-life dramas from the past which start young children off on a life-long quest on one particular person or event. Some examples might be Mary Queen of Scots, King Alfred, the traumatic experiences of Anne Frank, and the peaceful struggles for Indian Independence of Mahatma Ghandi. In a similar way, the bedtime story told or read to pre-school children can lead to the same interest in the past.

HISTORY FULFILS THE PRACTICAL NEEDS OF CHILDREN

If the past can help to foster the inward-looking and outward-looking needs of young children it can also supply practical needs through the use of concepts and skills specific to history. This is especially true of the sense of sequence or time. This involves a need for evidence so that children are always asking the question 'How do I know?' and looking for different types of evidence from artefacts (old objects), oral evidence, pictures, plans and maps, and written evidence (however slight). A sense of time is also concerned with change and difference through looking at different periods of the past in comparison with the present, although children in the primary years find the comparison between different historical periods, unrelated to the present, quite difficult to understand. Similarities can be found between different periods of the past because all periods are concerned with human beings and their feelings and motivations. We have altered relatively little through the ages. Study of the past reaches other concepts and ideas but sequence/time and change/difference are especially important and possible to instil into young children. Such understanding breaks down generation and racial barriers and helps to give children a feeling and respect for old objects. In spite of much previous research to the contrary,

the last fifteen years have shown that young children can begin to develop some sense of time.

A study of the past, with constant use of simple and then gradually more advanced sequence-lines leaving out dates, will give children aged between five and seven some idea of sequence (what comes before what). This can be developed, even at the age of six, into a beginners' time-line, using two, then more dates, and talking about 'centuries'. Exactly how many centuries can be understood by an eleven-year-old has yet to be researched.

Thus the past can mean many things to the young child: 'One is that *people* existed and *events* happened before I was born, that is five, six, seven, eight or more years ago. Another is that these existed and happened not only around me at home and at school, but in a much *wider world* (here there seems to be a link with the concept of place). Thirdly, these people and events *change* with time (e.g. growing old). Fourthly, the *present* (now) and the *past* (then) are *continuous* . . . Finally, the "past" is so huge that I find out about it in many ways: looking, feeling, talking, drawing, reading, writing. If a child of eleven realises that these five factors make up the past, he/she will have a wider and deeper understanding of him/herself in society' (Blyth, 1981).

How children learn about the past

It has yet to be discovered whether the National Curriculum helps children to learn about the past more successfully than history as part of topic work. How do they learn in topic work? Usually the topic title, rather than history, has dictated the content, unless it is a history-based theme. Therefore, content can become disconnected people and events spread over the whole of world history and studied over four years, and unless linked to a time-line, is usually forgotten except as an illustration of a theme. Too often the historical element is unimportant. If history is 'an enormous jigsaw with a lot of missing parts' (Carr, 1961), the missing parts are never found and the whole picture is never discovered by this method. In contrast, the National Curriculum helps learning by concentrating on historical topics more thoroughly. For example, one tomb or statue can start enquiry into other connecting events so that a wholeness and depth are given to learning. A statue of King Alfred in Wantage should lead to thinking about other historical happenings, as illustrated in Figure 1 opposite.

Children learn about the past in many different ways, some of which have been tested by the recent research outlines in Chapter 3. This book is not mainly concerned with methods of teaching the National Curriculum but with how teachers can manage the study units effectively without too much effort. Research and classroom experimentation have shown how certain approaches are successful with most children aged between five and seven.

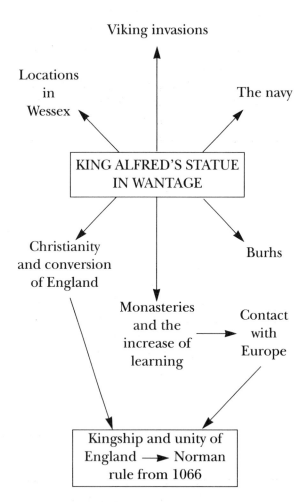

Figure 1 Links with King Alfred's statue in Wantage

PICTURE-READING

One under-used method is picture-reading from pictures in books, on posters, on television and in museums and art galleries. Close observation of a picture is started by the teacher asking the children to tell a story about what is happening in a certain picture and to sequence the 'events' in the picture. This in turn leads to children asking questions, and to a discussion with all participating. With older children this should encourage them to find out more about the picture and its story from books, other pictures and museums. Learning from the excellent television programmes specifically made for the National Curriculum is closely linked to picture-reading. The fact that a narrator explains the pictures on 'the small screen' makes the exercise less demanding, especially with the help of teachers' notes. However, teachers can become too dependent on these programmes and should not be guided too much by them. They should try to use more than one picture resource (see research by Swift and Jackson in Chapter 3). Picture-reading should be used in all the study units. For example, photographs are an excellent source for core units on 'Victorian Britain' and 'Britain since 1930'. Contemporary paintings, good artists' impressions and line-drawings as well as photographs of old maps are useful in all units. Susan Lynn's research (1993) shows that sequencing through picture-reading is an active and successful way of learning about the past (see Chapter 3 for more on Lynn's research and Chapter 9 for more on pictures).

ORAL INTERVIEWS

A second approach to help children with history is the use of oral interviews with older people ranging from about fifty to ninety years of age. Much advice has been given in publishers' packages and new method books about how children should conduct, tape-record and make use of interviews. This approach is particularly useful in Key Stage 1 but it can also be very pertinent in 'Britain since 1930' and Extension study B on local history. These last units need local old people to tell of life's experiences in their own and the children's locality. At present, little published research has been done on oral history in the primary school.

ACTIVE HISTORY

Primary teachers have no need to be told of the benefits of introducing different activities to help children to learn well. However, these activities should be purposely provided by the teacher, as history is naturally a narrative/story discipline leading to discussion rather than practical activities. The recent photocopiable sheets published by many well-known publishers in their packages of National Curriculum material provide specific activity; but teachers should guard against the 'old worksheet approach' dominating class activity. Handling artefacts (even if only reproduction), sequencing pictures, role-playing, going on visits, making history books with drawings and playing more intricate board games, as well as model making, are all good and well-tried activity methods. Set older juniors problems to solve, but give them the information with which to do so. All National Curriculum study units need activity methods, particularly Key Stage 1 and Year 3. So far no extensive research has been done on the success of historical role-playing on children's understanding of the past.

TEACHING STRATEGIES

Listening to the teacher is only one part of the whole area of teaching strategies. Others include various teaching styles, using materials and techniques appropriate to the child's stage of cognitive development. 'Where learning fails to take place, the fault lies not in the nature of the subject to be taught nor in the child, but in the form in which the learning experience is presented' (Fontana, 1984). These words emphasise the influence of the role of the teacher on the way children learn. Many teachers fail to 'match' tasks to each child's development, particularly as the year advances and differences between children's capabilities become more marked. Although Piaget's stages of cognitive development need not be adhered to strictly when dealing with the past, all children aged between five and eleven must work through the stages even if at different speeds, moving from preoperational schemes to concrete operational ones. To provide appropriate resources and teaching strategies, teachers should respond to children's classroom reactions which cannot usually be anticipated.

Listening to the teacher on the part of the child is closely linked with discussion between teacher and child which is a major way of learning in picture-reading. This is part of language development, though teachers should extend everyday, ordinary vocabulary to include specific historical words such as 'century', 'monarch' and 'artefact'. Two contemporary researchers, J. S. Bruner and Joan Tough, have encouraged teachers of young children to 'talk' to their children more, particularly in a one-to-one relationship, to ask leading questions and use the children's answers to promote thinking a step further. Bruner believes that, at about the age of six or seven, a child's language begins to be used in problem-solving and is not entirely dependent upon carrying out concrete operations. Joan Tough (Fontana, 1984) believes that 'there is no doubt that the development of language is dependent on the child's interaction with others'. Following the psychologist Vygotsky and his successors, she claims that 'naming' (putting words to objects) 'helped children to search for similarities and differences' and that 'words are central to the process of forming complex concepts'. Such concepts include change, sequence (time), evidence and power, all very relevant to teaching about the past. Story-telling by the teacher is another form of talking and discussion. This approach is ideal for children learning about far-away times, especially in Key Stage 1 when it is one of the few ways for children to learn about 'ways of life beyond living memory'. Well-told stories and readings from historical fiction are also good ways for all juniors to learn the 'magic of a well-told story' (Ministry of Education, 1952). In her research, Hilary Cooper emphasises the importance of discussion for concepts to be formed (see Chapter 3).

Older juniors learn about the past by reading and writing. The plethora of excellent books on the market since 1992 provides a feast of information (see Appendix 3). Differences in age range are beginning to be catered for, though not very successfully as yet. All study units of the National Curriculum benefit from children reading to find knowledge beyond that supplied by the teacher. Most juniors enjoy making, writing and illustrating their own history books. Hilary Cooper found that her eight-year-olds could use extracts from written evidence in contemporary sources.

Throughout the school years, we, as teachers, are trying to help our pupils to become thinking people. We need to bring children up to be thoughtful and critical of events around them. Peter Bryant and Margaret Donaldson believe that some kind of logical thinking begins in children much sooner than has been conventionally believed in the light of Piaget's experiments. Peter Bryant also believes that young children cannot reason easily because their memory is not normally exercised and they forget the knowledge which helps them to reason. Children learn to remember by repetition and reinforcement on the part of the teacher (Bryant, 1974; Donaldson, 1978). Thinking about the past should be encouraged as a way of learning and an antidote to too many inert facts. Children's historical knowledge outside school should be utilised and thought about. Thus teachers should discuss writing before it is done, and quality rather than quantity should be rewarded. All study units of the National Curriculum benefit from children being helped to think and reason through discussion.

Research and commentaries accessible to teachers, either before or after 1987, have not shown any short cut as to how young children learn best about the past. Linking this chapter and Chapter 3, I have tried to show where research has helped in many of the approaches. At present, therefore, there are no rigid 'rules' about learning history; learning depends on *ad hoc* opportunities presented in the classroom each day and therefore among young children, it is 'untidy' in accordance with a general pattern of growth.

Recent commentaries and research

The Final Report and Order of the National Curriculum in History (1991) did not seem to take account of the research carried out into primary history, although individual members of the Working Party had access to and may have read reports of relevant work. The National Curriculum in History will have to be 'based on a good measure of craft knowledge and guesswork' (Knight, 1989). But there is no list of sources consulted in either document. Let us hope that when changes are made, consultation with these specialists will have taken place. More inquiry should be carried out into how schools are reacting to the National Curriculum and how they would like it changed. In this chapter I consider work done since 1987, but the ongoing work of John West is still seminal. His unique ideas and practice have helped and influenced many researchers and teachers, particularly his use of time-lines (as clothes lines) across the classroom, and the telling of history stories.

If research and experiments can be explained in an accessible jargon-free language and shown to lead to suitable activities for children they are invaluable to teachers in three ways:

- They show what children are capable of doing and understanding, and therefore encourage teachers to try out work they thought was too difficult for children. Differentiation between tasks given to children and raised standards are constantly reiterated by researchers. For example, Peter Knight (1992) has shown that infants can understand and do enjoy learning about medieval times, contrary to teachers' widely held view that only three generations of the twentieth century is within children's understanding. He goes into more detail about how to read and learn about the legend of Robin Hood. This is very important as Robin Hood appears so frequently on children's and even adult's television programmes and an historian's approach is much needed.
- Secondly, research helps teachers to overcome the natural language problems associated with the past. Margaret Donaldson has shown that young children often do not respond to teachers' questions because they do not understand the adult historical language. For example, the Elizabethan Court could easily mean a law court and not the courtiers surrounding Elizabeth I.
- Thirdly, quite often the activities used by researchers to 'test' children prove enjoyable and part of good normal teaching outside the research activity.

The two major pieces of academic research since 1987 are those of Peter Knight and Hilary Cooper. Peter Knight (1989) was concerned with investigating the sense which children, aged six, eight, ten, twelve and fourteen, made of the actions of people in the past. Children of ten had no difficulty in offering explanations which showed understanding and did better than the 'control' group who had followed a conventional history course which had not encouraged them to look at people's motives and reasoning. For example, ten-year-olds had no difficulty in retelling a past story from the point of view of someone involved. Study of adults in the present was found to be as difficult for children to understand as study of adults in the medieval world. Like Hilary Cooper, he emphasised the need for teachers to discuss and explain history rather than present it as self-evident. He subsequently carried out work on twenty-eight primary teachers who were skilled in primary history work and, while noting a number of stimulating activities, failed to find much evidence that good history teaching was encouraging children to reason about the lives and actions of people in the past. Recently he has pointed to American research which shows that this is not just an English phenomenon (Knight, 1991–3).

Hilary Cooper (1992) was more concerned about children making inferences from sources. Her study investigated how, in doing this, children began to consider the possible feelings and thoughts of the people who made and used the pictures, artefacts, buildings, sites and documents. She found that learning to discuss key evidence as a class accelerated their activity to make deductions and inferences both in small group discussions when no adult was present, and in individual written answers.

A smaller piece of research undertaken by Susan Lynn (1993) was concerned with pictorial materials in infant and junior schools. In this, small groups of children aged six to seven and nine to eleven, few of whom had done any systematic history, were given packs of contemporary illustrations in various media (painting, engraving, etc.) to arrange in historical sequence after examining and discussing the pack contents. This activity potentially fulfils the needs of the Attainment Target. From this, we learn that most children of both age groups understand the concept of historical sequencing at about level 1, ('ability to sequence events and objects'), but were more comfortable with a very long time span than a short one. Apart from the impulsive

thinkers, children of both age groups tried to reason historically by drawing on historical knowledge they thought they had. Leaving aside the limitations of historical knowledge and language, their difficulties stemmed from lack of practice in looking carefully at pictures and from some very common misconceptions about the past. For example, they thought that until modern times, 'there were no bright colours'. The research points to a need to teach careful observations of pictures and for 'buzz' sessions (talking to children) to draw on both children's knowledge of the past gained outside school and any major misconceptions.

Apart from academic research, the findings of which tend to be remote for teachers, national and local surveys have been undertaken using, in the main, questionnaires to teachers, rather than classroom contact. Sometimes teachers express children's likes and understandings of the past from their stereotype of what they think children *should* like and can understand rather than what they actually do! Therefore, more can be read into these surveys than should be. The Department of History at Chester College made a survey of thirty-four schools in Chester, North Cheshire and Wirral between 1985 and 1987 (Swift and Jackson, 1987). This was very thorough and the findings were a microcosm of the state of history made public by the Department of Education and Science in *The Teaching of History and Geography* (DES, 1989). Both showed that teachers did not know what history as a discipline meant and that clear planning of the whole primary curriculum was lacking. Together with lack of resources, this threw teachers into undigested television programmes and formal exposition of historical facts. These failings had already been noticed by HMI in 1978 and 1985 and had not been corrected probably because history was viewed as a 'Cinderella' subject in the primary school. Therefore the need for a National Curriculum was clearly evident.

In addition to research and surveys, teachers can benefit from books on how to teach history.

Between 1987 and 1991 there was a dearth of such books for primary teachers. However, there are exceptions. Henry Pluckrose's *Children learning History* (Pluckrose, 1991) was written when the Final Report had been published but before the Final Order. It is a general book from a lifetime's experience and takes notice of some recent research. The other two books are a new edition of my *History in Primary Schools* (Blyth, 1989 and 1990) and *History 5 to 9* (Blyth, 1988), which are mainly classroom activity books, the latter incorporating my research at the Froebel Educational Institute (1983–5). Therefore the mass of publications which came out in 1992 are welcome additions, though may of necessity, have been written with undue haste.

At present, four very different publications are available. *Practical Guides: History* (Hill and Morris, 1991) tries valiantly to cover the ground, providing material and teaching ideas for all the eight units of Key Stage 2, as well as Key Stage 1. It is very good on activities for Key Stage 1 and how history could figure in school assemblies, using humorous sketches and photographs to relieve the printed page; but the knowledge is rather superficial on the Extension studies in Key Stage 2 and has one or two factual inaccuracies. A bibliography would also have been helpful. *History at Key Stages 1 and 2* (Knight, 1991) is a quick guide to the History National Curriculum to get teachers started. It is a compact and well-written book, though subjective in viewpoint, and is presented in a racy, readable style. The contemporary pictures and apt quotations at the beginning of each chapter are instructive and amusing. This would be worth a second edition if any changes are made in the National Curriculum and when schools have experienced the early years of implementation.

The Really Practical Guide to Primary History (Wright, 1992) is neither a solid resource book, nor an inspirational canter but a book full of practical tasks for children, as the title suggests, and linked to the National Curriculum. It is well set out with plenty of black and white photographs, sketches, plans and diagrams. Unfortunately, there are no references or bibliography, and it therefore tends to be a temporary guide to the present National Curriculum rather than a book suitable for a second edition. *The Teaching of History* (Cooper, 1992) is a cross between a description of her own research and detailed teaching techniques from her own experience. The National Curriculum seems to be belatedly introduced to make the book topical. It will be very useful for teacher trainers and students undertaking work for dissertations. Hilary Cooper's understanding of history as a discipline and her wide experience in primary schools shines through the pages. A second edition, considered in tranquillity, might become a 'classic' in this sphere.

The implementation of the National Curriculum and publication of more research and commentaries, as outlined in this chapter, should help to ensure the larger presence and quality teaching of history in primary schools in the coming years.

PART II

A closer look at history in the National Curriculum

The Attainment Target at Key Stages 1 and 2

Most teachers have been concerned with mastering the content of the units of study chosen for their class. The time involved in preparing and teaching these units is considerable, and the 1994 Proposals encourage teachers to plan some units in outline and parts of them in detail. Encouraging teachers to choose units precludes any assessment of children on detailed historical facts, which is as it should be.

The 1994 Dearing Proposals state that the units of study are central in National Curriculum History. In history there are no nationally-prescribed tests, although the National Curriculum Council (NCC) has already suggested tests for teachers to use with seven-year-olds at Key Stage 1 (January 1993). The School Curriculum and Assessment Authority (SCAA) will publish material to show how the new 'level descriptions' will work.

While preparing content and methods of teaching for a specific unit of study, teachers should check that as many as possible of the 'level descriptions' are introduced and that activities are set according to the Final Order (January 1995). However, the idea of assessing young children's progress in historical thinking by 'levels' has been refuted as unhistorical by some researchers Martin Booth (1993) writes of the (then) Attainment Targets: '. . . their defects as a

framework for charting the nature and development of children's thinking are manifold' since history is a problem-solving discipline, not a progressive one. It is to be hoped that the levels will be used by teachers rather than the teachers being dominated by them.

The Attainment Target introduced by the 1994 Proposals incorporates the content of all three previous targets: knowledge, understanding and skills. Therefore the interpretation of history and use of historical sources spelled out in the old AT2 and AT3 have become part of 'skills'. This single target is explained in the last part of the 1994 Proposals in the section on 'progression' (pp. iv–v).

Together with this simplification, the statements of attainment become 'level descriptions' for assessment at the end of each key stage. A new welcome emphasis, previously omitted from the history curriculum, is 'the ability to communicate knowledge and understanding', which includes children's written, oral and visual work. The 'level descriptions' are on pp. 14–15 in the 1994 Proposals. As before, Key Stage 1 children are expected to be assessed on levels 1 to 3, and Key Stage 2 children on levels 2 to 5. Children must show factual knowledge of people and events, including dates from level 4 onwards.

WHAT USE IS THE NON-STATUTORY GUIDANCE OF 1991?

The statements of attainment in the Final Order and Non-Statutory Guidance of 1991 are still useful for reference, particularly if teachers have become accustomed to them. Therefore reference should still be made to the 1991 publications where helpful. For example, Diagram 2 on the back of page B3 is a summary chart detailing groups of concepts (strands) concerned with knowledge and understanding.

The first strand is 'change and continuity', which includes the first statements at each level from 1 to 5. In each case they are labelled (a). This strand emphasises that history is concerned with change, that there are different kinds of change (gradual/rapid and local/national) and that change can vary in different periods of the past. In discussion, teachers should try to get across that change is not always progress; that different people see change in different ways; and that learning the language of change is important. For instance, vocabulary such as:

century, BC and AD, and names for periods of the past should be introduced.

The second strand is 'causes and consequences', which includes the second statements (b) at each level of attainment, all including the word 'reason'. This strand aims to emphasise different kinds of cause and consequence, that they may vary in importance; that their links can be complex; and that people are key factors.

The third strand (c) is concerned with different 'features' in a different time, in order to highlight people's ideas and how societies functioned. Thus social life plays a large part in this strand; aspects of life in Tudor Britain would include different social classes, life in town and country, costume, travel and houses. In spite of all these detailed recommendations, the Non-Statutory Guidance (1991) offers some consolation in that teachers are not expected to cover all these areas!

DEVELOPING CHILDREN'S VIEWS ON HISTORY

History is, in the first place, what actually happened in the past. Most of us do not know what happened until research slowly builds up a new picture. History is also views (interpretations) written in books or expressed orally, which may or may not be true, particularly if certain facts are omitted. Some people use history to influence readers politically or socially, as do the media. Children should be trained to view the printed word and what is said orally with caution and to consider more than one book or point of view. Since children are likely to read only one book, teachers must discuss the views or omissions of facts with them. Different views make the past interesting but children, like many adults, tend to seek 'one right view' which seems to make

understanding easier for them. Children should make their own interpretations of the past, and know the differences between fact and fiction. Some stories are untrue; some may have some truth in them; and some are true. Differences in interpretation also apply to different versions of the same event: Thomas Cromwell (a minister of Henry VIII) gave a different account of a visit to a monastery than that given by the abbot at the time of the dissolution of the monasteries (1536–9). Thomas Cromwell wanted to close monasteries to satisfy the will of his master Henry VIII; the abbots naturally did not want this to happen. As documentation of such an event is almost bound to be partial in two senses, biased but also incomplete, a true account is virtually impossible to find. We are also concerned with lack of evidence for a given event. Children should also learn to distinguish between a fact and a point of view. That Henry VIII had Sir Thomas More executed is a fact. Whether More was a saint or a traitor, is a point of view.

Pictures, either contemporary, created later, or made by artists today, can tell a false story, often through lack of evidence. Hans Holbein's portraits of Henry VIII depict him as an all-powerful strong man. Portraits of Elizabeth I always made her appear young. Van Dyck depicted Charles II on horseback, or waist upwards, to disguise his small stature. Popular stereotypes can also distort history. Oliver Cromwell supported the rights of individuals (freedom) against the absolute rule of Charles I, yet turned out to be as great a dictator, dissolving Parliament as Charles had done, and ruthlessly subjecting Ireland to English rule.

Children should be aware of the many contemporary views of an event or person in the past, as well as many present-day views of the same event. A detailed example of eight-year-olds using different written views of a person in the past is given in *Teaching Attainment Target 2 in National Curriculum History* (Fines and Hopkins, 1992). These viewpoints on King Richard III (slightly more appropriate to Key Stage III: Medieval Realms) come from a writer in the following century (sixteenth); a nineteenth-century historian; and a modern historian. More easily understood in Key Stage 2 would be the contemporary views of children working in nineteenth-century factories: the written reports of factory commissioners giving views of children complaining about their treatment, and those of factory owners justifying their need to remain profitable.

Children should also look at present-day interpretations of the past and compare them with each other. The NCC funded a project conducted by Bromley and Dorset Local Education Authorities to fulfil the aims of the 1991 Final Order 'to develop awareness of different ways of representing past events'. They used modern advertisements, theme parks, computer simulations, videos, films, TV programmes and oral history to give different views of one past event. For example the evacuation of children during World War II can be interpreted differently by a TV programme and by one old person who experienced it. Written evidence and pictures were the only ways to give interpretations in earlier centuries when visual technology did not exist or was in its infancy.

CHOOSING HISTORICAL SOURCES

Teachers should find suitable sources for children to use on a given topic. These sources may include artefacts, contemporary pictures, films, tapes of oral discussions, buildings or written documents. Before 1066 most extant sources are archaeological or written in Latin or Anglo-Saxon. Tudor and Stuart handwriting (palaeography) is difficult to read though written in fairly comprehensible English: transcriptions are often available from record offices. After 1700 handwriting became clearer and most children aged nine to eleven can read Victorian 'copperplate' more easily than twentieth-century handwriting! When sources are understood and the content unravelled, then teachers should help children to evaluate them and place these sources in historical context. Thus, the tacit assumptions of each period according to the political, economic, technological, scientific, social, religious and cultural perspectives (p. 3 of the

1994 Proposals) have to be known. At present, written sources are more inaccessible to teachers than other sources. Bishop Asser's *Life of King Alfred,* the king of Wessex in the ninth century A.D., is heavily biased in favour of Alfred, who may not now be considered as 'great' as Asser made out. (Why did he do that?) Queen Victoria's letters give a perfect image of Prince Albert. Knowing the bias of such written sources should help teachers and children to learn about the past from them ('draw inferences from them') to create their own time-picture. Older children should be using more than one source, and sources of different kinds, for example oral, pictorial and written. More will be said about the single Attainment Target in Chapter 10, which looks at assessment.

Key Stage 1 – Programme of study

One of the most innovative features of the History National Curriculum is the inclusion of history for five- to seven-year-olds. Thus, children becoming five during the Reception year should be included in this study unit. The programme has two parts. The first is family, oral and local history. The second is the more distant past – 'the way of life of people beyond living memory'. As most people aged seventy and over can only remember back to 1920, this second part means any part of the past in Britain or elsewhere from 1920 back to the Stone Age which is appropriate for infants. The choice of topic here is obviously vast and teachers must make their own decisions based on what interests them and what resources are available. For many years successful work has been done on family history, oral history and artefacts. Since the National Curriculum became law, a profusion of excellent books set in the twentieth century and suitable for infants has been published. So effective are many of these books that teachers have been tempted to overlook the second part of the unit before 1900. So far, few publishers have produced suitable material for this period of the past. Nor has there been much discussion as to when to introduce such topics in the three years. The following section will provide some ideas for structuring history for the three years of the infant school.

RECEPTION (FOUR- TO FIVE-YEAR-OLDS)

I have drawn on Paul Bish's work with nursery children in this part of the chapter, as well as adding to his work on time-lines and toys with other approaches familiarising very young children with the existence of 'the past'. Historical language can be used very early on with the teacher introducing the words 'old', 'a long time ago', 'when you were a baby' and 'yesterday'. They should be repeated and constantly discussed as to meaning. The passage of time can be started, not only from learning to tell the time from a large-faced cardboard clock with numbers and hands, but also by making days of the week cards which should be displayed each day and repeated every week. Children should be asked to put them in sequence. The four seasons and months of the year are a development of this, using colourful calendars for the year concerned. The date of the year concerned (for example, 1994) should always be on display. A class diary may be kept on the notice-board naming one 'event' each day of the week.

These are spasmodic approaches to time and the past. A more positively historical approach is one in which pictures are used (treated in more detail in Chapter 9). Picture work can be started early with a favourite story-time book such as *Peepo* (Janet and Allan Ahlberg, Picture Puffin, 1983).

This book looks at life today from a baby's point of view and is a good start for family history later in the infant years. Picture-reading through discussion is the most potent source of learning about the past at this stage. Artists' impressions can be misleading in content and colour, and cartoons may easily provide laughter rather than understanding. Collaboration between artist and historian is the ideal situation. Contemporary paintings give details which interest young children, but some may be too 'cluttered' on the page for limited concentration. Clear, large photographs of nineteenth- and twentieth-century people and events are always a success. Pictures and posters of any period of the past can help to provide an historical awareness.

Nursery rhymes and fairy tales all provide an 'old world' timeless atmosphere in clothes, houses and vehicles (usually horses!) with an emphasis on royalty. Kings, queens, princes and princesses are taken for granted. In *Sleeping Beauty* (Ladybird, 1990), a princess and daughter of a king and queen, falls asleep for one hundred years. *Cinderella* meets a prince and *Old King Cole* is a king and a 'merry' one at that! It may be too early to discuss whether these stories are true or not, but comparisons can be made between 'then' and 'now'; for instance 'once upon a time' is always in the past. Sequencing events in the stories by discussion and using pictures in the story book makes an early start to the more purposeful sequencing of their own lives on short time-lines in the next two years.

The 'Wendy house', renamed 'home-corner', can be the centre for role-playing of rooms from another age (for example, a kitchen), a picnic for Elizabeth I on a 'Progress', Alfred 'burning the cakes' in a Saxon cottage and the 'coronation' of William I in Westminster Abbey. Teachers should discuss beforehand the people involved, the 'stage' properties required and what actually happened. Another practical approach is having a 'history' table, as a change from a nature table. Teachers and children could bring old objects to place on the table – perhaps one group of children each week – with a varying emphasis on kitchen utensils, clothes, toys or books. Discussion about 'how old', 'what was it used for' and 'what does it tell us about the past' should lead to the teacher labelling each artefact with a name.

All these approaches will be spasmodic and will depend upon opportunities offered by other work. Any or all of these suggestions may be taken up. The Year 1 infant teacher should know what approaches have been used in Reception to link with the more systematic work on family and oral history and artefacts in Years 1 and 2. Paul Bish of Bishops' Hull County Primary School, Taunton, describes his work with Reception children below.

Building a sense of time-passing, change and continuity in Reception children

Reception children are exempt from the need to follow the National Curriculum until they reach the age of five. However, I believe that appropriately targeted activities can build on children's own natural curiosity about the world around them to begin to develop historical skills and concepts. Most successful work in Key Stage 1 begins from the children's direct experience and broadens out. This is particularly true of work with Reception children.

During the Spring Term of 1993 my class of twenty-four Reception children have been following the topic of 'change'. This has proved to be a good stimulus for work across the curriculum. The topic has obvious potential for historical work, and I therefore planned it into a series of activities which I hoped would provoke historical understanding. My objectives with these activities were to encourage the children to use appropriate historical language, such as 'old', 'new', 'before' and 'after'; to begin to foster an idea of change over time, firstly through themselves changing and then through the study of artefacts; and to foster an idea of continuity by children coming to realise that their parents were once their age, and that they themselves will grow up into adults and have memories of childhood.

Ourselves changing

After a series of discussions, the children completed three time-line activities. Two of the time-lines were completed over several days to maintain interest and concentration. The children worked in small groups supervised by myself and my nursery nurse, Sylvia Handscombe. The last was completed in one session, as an assessment activity.

The first time-line concerned the pattern of the children's day. We discussed what we did on getting up, going to school, coming home and at bedtime. After four pictures were completed, the children were asked to sequence them in the correct order and they were stuck into a zig-zag book. All the children achieved this with varying amounts of guidance. Some successfully ordered them on the table but stuck them into the zig-zag books in the wrong order.

The second time-line concerned their personal history. We looked at photographs of babies, toddlers and school-aged children. Some children brought photographs of themselves into school. I showed photographs of myself as a child. We talked of what we could do at each age. Pictures were drawn to record these discussions, then sequenced and stuck onto a time-line. The children found this activity much easier than the first one, perhaps because there were only three pictures instead of four and there was a more obvious 'right' order. This activity would have been best done before the first one.

The final time-line concerned the children themselves as babies, as they were now, and as a 'grown up'. Each child was given a strip of paper divided into three sections. I asked them to draw themselves as a baby in the first one, and as they are now in the second one. I then asked what they would like to be when they 'grow up', like their parents. This was not easily understood by many of the children. When one child mentioned that she wanted to be a nurse, they all followed

suit! Either I had failed to explain myself clearly or the concept of a 'job' was beyond the children's development. All the time-line activities provoked interesting discussions and historical language was used by the children without prompting. The children demonstrated an ability to sequence events in a correct time order, and obviously understood that they themselves were changing and growing over time.

Toys

The children brought their favourite toys into school and we discussed how they had acquired them and why they were special. We then used them for sorting and language activities. We next discussed toys the children had when they were younger, and toys which older brothers and sisters might play with. I then showed them a collection of toys which we sorted into toys for babies and toddlers, toys for 'our' age and toys for older brothers and sisters. Some toys were hard to place and were appropriate for more than one age group. To record this activity, the children cut out pictures of toys from magazines and catalogues and sequenced them appropriately.

Some parents brought their own childhood toys and talked about them with the children. One parent kindly trusted us with his precious 1950s tinplate tanks and clockwork train, all in excellent condition. We compared these with modern equivalents and noticed the different materials and motive power. Even though they had been discussing the clockwork train and knew that it had belonged to Robert's father when he was a boy, they still described it as 'new' because of its pristine condition, whilst a class toy, a rather battered plastic tractor, was described as 'old'.

I used a 'Child Education' poster of a Victorian nursery to stimulate discussion on similarities and differences between the toys on the poster and those the children had at home. Similarities were noticed most, and many of the toys were similar to modern dolls and puzzles. Differences were subtle and not easily discernible from a poster. It would have been much more useful to have had genuine artefacts to handle. Some children did notice the lack of cars, aeroplanes, spaceships, etc., and several guessed that this was because they had not been invented 'in the old days'. This I felt was a concrete example of a growing historical understanding.

Taken as a whole, I consider that these activities did achieve the objectives I set out at the beginning of the topic. Certainly the need for activities to be directly related to the children's experience was very apparent. The need for real objects rather than abstractions was also strongly demonstrated. The most successful activities included these two elements. However, I feel that a good foundation has been laid for future historical work and that young children can have quite a sophisticated understanding of the time component of their world.

YEARS 1 AND 2 (FIVE-, SIX- AND SEVEN-YEAR-OLDS)

In the same way that much infant teaching is geared to language and number, so the approach to the National Curriculum in History should be cross-curricular and not done at any particular time of the week, though there should be some history done each week. As children enter the infant school at age five and often in different terms throughout the year, teaching plans must remain very flexible. Teachers should check with the 1995 Final Order to see that they are covering the main suggestions. The child and family are the first topic, but recent publications (notably from Ginn, Longman, Oxford University Press and Scholastic) have broadened out this theme and added toys, holidays, celebrations and school life. Each theme should lead to the completion of a small backwards time-line into the past with pictures in sequence underneath important dates (see the 'Changing Times' series from Franklin Watts, 1992).

Teachers should get clear in their own minds the differences between types of stories and try to convey these to children when some stories have been told. The following interpretations may help:

- Fictional stories using the past (any parts of historical fiction, e.g. D. Rees *The House That Moved*, Puffin, 1982).

- A story of true events (e.g. Guy Fawkes and the Gunpowder Plot).
- A legend with some evidence that it is true (e.g. Robin Hood, King Arthur, Dick Whittington).
- A myth handed down by oral tradition which cannot be accurately placed in time, if at all (e.g. classical heroes and heroines, Persephone, Theseus and the Minotaur, Romulus and Remus, The Wooden Horse, St George and the Dragon).

The main difference is that true stories can be dated in the teacher's mind and put on a time-line. Myths and legends are less tied to time, but time is the essence of history. Concepts of the 'underworld', 'heroes', 'monsters' and 'giants' are unfamiliar except in fairy stories in which real life is exaggerated as good or bad. Therefore they should be approached by teachers with caution.

Stories should be told (not read) if possible in all infant years, but are an essential approach for the first two terms of Year 2 when 'a period of the past beyond living memory' is studied. They are best centred around an important person or event (e.g. King Alfred of Wessex or the Armada) and put on a time-line. Teachers will have to make up their own stories from junior reading books until suitable stories are published for infants to read.

As a link with Key Stage 2, the first half of the last term could well be spent on a mini topic of in-depth work involving a visit to a related place. This should prepare Year 2 infants for the more formal approach of 'Romans, Anglo-Saxons and Vikings in Britain' or 'Victorian Britain'. It is as well to concentrate on medieval British History, as this is omitted from Key Stage 2. Themes suggested are Robin Hood, life in a castle, the local parish church, the Canterbury pilgrims and their stories (Ian Serailler *The Road to Canterbury*, Heinemann, 1981; and Alison and Michael Bagenal *This Merry Company*, OUP, 1979), King Arthur and his knights, and children in the Tower of London. Mini-topics from later periods might include the Tudor ship *Mary Rose*, a famous local family and their house, and the Edwardians (1901–10), omitted from Key Stage 2. This mini-topic is likely to dominate this part of the term, and other parts of the curriculum should therefore be related to it.

Many different methods of approach can be used to study this content. The methods already suggested for the Reception class should be continued and more structured work done on artefacts and oral history. Artefacts are concrete evidence of all periods of the past. Most of them come from the years since 1945, but antique shops do sell small objects as far back as Victorian times. Archaeological remains usually represent time before the Norman Conquest, but there are few genuine artefacts for the years 1066 to 1880. Replicas are made for all periods and teachers should discuss the meaning of the word 'replica'. There is a progression in methods of approach. In the first place, a teacher should bring his or her own personal objects in a small suitcase/zip bag. The children should be encouraged to ask questions about the objects and what sort of person might own the bag. Secondly, an object can be put in a 'feely' bag or bags, with children guessing what the object might be, using touch alone. Then a list of questions could be put to the children to answer about the object in order for them to reach the correct answer. The third

method is to divide the class into groups and let each group study one object and answer the same questions prepared by the teacher. Artefacts could change groups and each group could tape-record their discussions. The teacher should lead the final whole-class discussion when all ideas would be pooled. Overall conclusions could be put on the blackboard and objects, or drawings of them, on a large class time-line.

Oral history and the use of older people in interviews has also been a tried method of approach, particularly if the same people can be used for several years to represent different decades, i.e. sixty-year-olds, seventy-year-olds and eighty-year-olds. Thus social life in the locality in the 1910s, 1920s and 1930s has a natural source of evidence. Grannies and grandads may have been over-used and other older people are just as useful, though they do not relate so easily to the children's family trees. Children should prepare leading questions, have them written down (quite an effort for infants) and practise using the tape-recorder. Several older people for several groups of children is the best way to gain most information and keep all the children involved. Topics for an interview can include all aspects of social life – family, home, job, clothes, shopping, food, leisure and holidays, games, school, buses and all forms of transport. Interviewees should be asked which topic(s) they prefer to talk about. When the visitors have gone, all the tapes should be played with the teacher helping the children to agree the common information from all of them on a certain topic. At the very end, the teacher might tape-record the summary result, replay it to the children and send a copy to each visitor as a memento of their visit.

These suggestions are personal ones. Three publications should reinforce them. One is the Final Order and Non-Statutory Guidance for Wales. Figure 2 shows a simplified version of the Key Stage 1 Topic Checklist, and Figure 3 shows a chart to develop a sense of chronology at Key Stage 1 through time-lines. The second publication is the *Standard Assessment Tasks for Key*

Figure 2 Key Stage 1 Topic Checklist

Taking the key stage as a whole, will the selected themes and topics provide opportunities to deal with:

- change over time, for example, since grandparents' days ☐
- the lives of famous people in the past ☐
- everyday life in the past ☐
- myths and legends, including those from Wales ☐
- stories about historical events in the past ☐
- fictional stories set in the past including those about Wales and Welsh people ☐
- eye-witness accounts ☐
- the past beyond living memory ☐

Will pupils have opportunities to:

- use a range of sources, e.g. photographs, artefacts, songs ☐
- ask questions about the past ☐

© Curriculum Council for Wales 1991

Figure 3 The Development of a Sense of Chronology at Key Stage 1 through a series of time-lines

Non-Written
artefacts/pictures of artefacts/pictures of people at various ages/same person at different ages
All the above can be put into a chronological sequence.

Day Line

| Bed | School starts | Playtime | Lunch | School ends | Bed |

Clock faces to be filled in. Use the day line over a period of time. Progress to year line.

Year Line

Jan   Dec

There are other ways of dividing the year which teachers may wish to investigate (e.g. seasons).

Child's Time-Line (RETROGRAPH)

This Year	Last Year	2 Years Ago	3 Years Ago	4 Years Ago	5 Years Ago	6 Years Ago	
	broke leg	started school	baby sister born	first walked	first tooth	born	Extended using teachers own information, or that of other adults

Century Line

© Curriculum Council for Wales 1991

Stage 1 History for seven-year-olds, published in January 1993. This consists of a teachers' handbook and booklets on 'stories', 'photographs', 'objects' and 'change in history', giving detailed help to teachers testing children at levels 1 to 3 of the level descriptions. These booklets give examples of activities for teachers to use in their day-to-day teaching, as well as examples for the formulation of tests of their own material (see Chapter 10 for more details). The third publication is *Teaching History in Key Stage 1* from the National Curriculum Council. This shows how different elements of the programme of study can help progression in learning and how challenging time-lines and sequencing activities can develop a sense of chronology.

Key Stage 2 – Programme of study: Core units

Two overriding considerations dominate the National Curriculum in History. One is that children should understand and be able to use chronology to gain a sense of time. At first it was laid down that the core units should be taught in correct chronological order. The other consideration is that the main outline of British history from the Romans in Britain (first century AD) to the present day should form the content. This is known as the 'British Heritage', particularly emphasising British successes and outstanding personalities. Therefore two out of the four compulsory core units span British history from Roman times to 1714 except for medieval history (c.1066–c.1485) which is reserved for Key Stage 3. The alternative of 'Victorian Britain' or 'Britain since 1930' is the final part of the British core units. This is a wise decision as much of the twentieth-century content will get some attention in Key Stage 1, and many schools already spend a lot of time on Victorian Britain. The other compulsory unit – 'Ancient Greece' – represents the study of an ancient civilisation different from most children's experience.

Teachers have been overpowered by the preparation involved in these units, partly because many of them have been brought up on topic work which was not concerned with chronology or a systematic study of historical events and characters through time. The assurance that not all parts of the programmes need to be studied in equal depth has not yet lifted the feelings of pressure, as many teachers do not know which parts to select to make historical sense. In-service education of teachers (INSET) should be able to lead the way in helping with these decisions, though accessibility of suitable resources may be the final deciding factor. This flexibility is welcome as long as a time-line and/or family tree is used to fill in the main gaps through discussion. Therefore teachers need to be recommended scholarly yet lively and well-illustrated books for use by children in Key Stage 3 as reading books, as well as providing quick background reading for the teachers themselves. I strongly recommend Longman's 'Then and There' series.

The core units may be taught as separate history-based topics, notably 'Life in Tudor Times'. Others can be more easily integrated into a cross-curricular approach, notably 'Romans, Anglo-Saxons and Vikings in Britain' and 'Britain since 1930'. The Non-Statutory Guidance (1991) gives a list of the needs of the PESCR formula. This should enable political, economic, social, religious and cultural emphases to be considered in all programmes in varying degrees. For example, political and social emphases are easily catered for in 'Life in Tudor Times' whereas economic history figures largely in 'Victorian Britain' and 'Britain since 1930'. Multicultural and gender issues are natural discussion points in Core unit 1 and 'Britain since 1930'. It is often more difficult to include the histories of Ireland, Wales and Scotland, though obvious references include the Roman invasion into Wales (before the defeat of Boudicca), Henry VII as a Tudor

(Welsh) prince, Mary Queen of Scots' (and of France at one time) arrival in England in 1567 and Queen Victoria's building of Balmoral Castle. A certain knowledge of Welsh, Irish and Scottish history is needed to clarify the connection between English history and these events, some of which are crucially important for the development of British history.

ROMANS, ANGLO-SAXONS AND VIKINGS IN BRITAIN (KEY STAGE 2: CORE UNIT 1)

This compulsory core unit is deceptive so far as preparation of material is concerned. The Romans and Vikings have been used regularly in topic work to cater for children's love of powerful warriors, ships and battles. But to study one of three is not the same thing as looking at them all at once, or part of the concept of invasions and settlers in Britain leading to our own special mixture of different races. When the Anglo-Saxons are added and they become one unit, the pre-National Curriculum has been altered considerably.

To undertake this work in one term or less is a daunting task. Therefore, the original plan of the Interim Report of 1990 to cover all three invaders with the same depth has been reconsidered, and now the programme of study advocates concentration on one. Many teachers will choose to concentrate on Romans or Vikings and use a published pupil's reading book as a basis of knowledge. I will mention all three but will go into more detail about the Anglo-Saxons.

Many teachers and most publishers have presumed that this unit should be studied in Year 3 – being the first of the chronology of British history. However, it might be more appropriate to study it in Year 5 or 6 when children have a better understanding of historical concepts. To me, the Victorian or twentieth-century units are a more suitable transition from Key Stage 1. Reasons for this are many. In terms of the length of time required to study it, unit 1 is the longest of the core units, one thousand years from 55 BC (Julius Caesar's landing) to King Canute (from Denmark) in 1035. It is tantalising for primary teachers that *the* big invasion of 1066 is forbidden territory as it comes into Key Stage 3. Therefore we 'make do' with the less exciting and well-documented invasions of our island. This period is as long as any Extension study A included to show a line of development and change over time; only this unit does not concentrate on one theme, it is concerned with the wars, social life, religious life, archaeological remains, ships and transport of three different European peoples. The constant use of time-lines is essential.

Another reason is that a feeling for place is needed from the beginning, and in 55 BC there was no such thing as 'England' geographically, but it is hoped that by the time this unit is studied children will know how to look at a map of Britain. Celtic Britain was divided up into tribes, each of which was willing to cooperate with an invader to defy their local enemies, at least until they wanted to become 'settlers'. There was no national awareness and the invaders made the most of this. Only towards the end of the period did Wessex lead these kingdoms into some sort of unity, but by 1066 William the Conqueror could raise old quarrels for his own ends.

Linked to this geographical need is the fact that the invaders came from unheard of lands – Italy, Norway, Sweden, Denmark and northern Germany – presenting language difficulties. Where are these lands and how far away are they? Another long look at a simple atlas, this time of Europe, is needed, though the Geography National Curriculum does not advocate this as early as Year 3. The Vikings also had contact with America, Iceland and Greenland. Where are they? It is good for children to know that Britain was part of the Roman Empire (55 BC to c.400 AD), but what is an 'empire' and how extensive was the famous Roman one? This is bound to bring in North Africa and other Mediterranean lands.

Another point to bear in mind is that the first century AD is so far away in time that it is difficult to find out enough information about personalities, even from the few written sources. We strive to give some idea to our pupils of Boudicca, the rebel queen of the Iceni tribe in East Anglia, King Alfred, fighter/idealist of Wessex, the Saxon leader Byrhtnoth defeated by the Vikings at the Battle of Maldon (991 AD), St Augustine preaching to King Ethelbert of Kent and Abbess Hilda founder of the famous mixed monastery at Whitby. But we cannot give the colourful, personal details, so engaging to primary children, which are more readily available in later periods of British history.

Therefore teachers brave enough to take on this unit with seven-year-olds have a historical challenge ahead of them. However, it does illustrate change over a long period of time, it is intrinsically multicultural and the PESCR formula is easy to introduce. It covers geographical work naturally, as well as all sorts of different types of evidence, such as place names, archaeology, written sources, visits to places of interest and many others.

Romans

The Romans came to Britain in 55 BC and withdrew to defend their crumbling empire about 400 AD. During that time they were certainly military invaders but only those who married Britons settled and became Romano-British. A study of this part of the unit should start with the Celts in Britain and the Romans in the Roman Empire. It divides itself up neatly into four topics: the invasion and conquest, Roman roads, forts

and Hadrian's Wall; Boudicca's rebellion and defeat; Roman towns, trade and villas; Roman and British gods and goddesses and the beginning of Christianity. Each is well documented in many suitable books and other resources, and the topic lends itself to good activities for primary children such as making models of towns and villas, making mosaic pictures and deciphering writing on Roman tombstones. The map of roads in Roman Britain, punctured by fortified towns such as London, York, Chester, Lincoln and St Albans represents the matter-of-fact clarity of the Roman mind and experience in Britain. There seem to be few Roman personalities except distant Emperors (Claudius and Hadrian) who ordered things to be done but who only paid flying visits to Britain, if at all. The Romans seem to be super-efficient and hard working, but there are few signs of individualism or personal feelings.

More important than the Romans being in Britain, as few stayed, is what they left behind. These include roads, buildings such as Porchester Castle, Fishbourne Palace and the baths at Bath, as well as Hadrian's Wall and its milecastles, signal towers and forts, the Roman walls to towns such as Chester and the villas with central heating (hypocausts). Names of towns and other English words come from Latin and the Roman occupation. Styles of architecture also came from Rome; the columns of the entrance to the British Museum are an example. Smaller items displayed in museums (and still being found) also provide evidence of Roman settlement. The legacy in evidence in the country is more important than Roman events and people in a 'broad brush' treatment.

Anglo-Saxons

This period of c.500 to 900 AD is the least well known in unit 1, yet in many ways it is the richest historically. The Anglo-Saxons came from north Germany, Denmark and what is now Holland and Belgium. Known as 'Barbarians', they attacked the Roman Empire. British kings asked them to come to Britain to help them against their internal enemies after the Romans had left. But the Saxons would not go home and eventually made Roman Britain into 'England'. These four hundred years are represented by colourful characters, such as the legendary King Arthur, King Offa of Mercia (central England), the saints who converted England to Christianity and above all King Alfred of Wessex. There are many buildings and remains as well as beautiful artefacts which represent the civilization of the Saxon period. Besides this material evidence, there are several readable written sources, now translated from Latin/Saxon into English. They are simple accounts and easy to understand. The two most famous and easily accessible are *The Anglo-Saxon Chronicle* and the Venerable Bede's *Ecclesiastical History of the English Nation*, the first history of England.

King Arthur of Round Table fame is a legend as well as a myth. Historically, Arthur is a shadowy figure, but many exciting stories suitable for children surround his name. He was a British king about the time of the fall of the Roman Empire when Roman soldiers were leaving England. In his *In Search of the Dark Ages* Michael Wood (1981) writes 'There is no myth in British history, and few in the world, to match the story of King Arthur and the Knights of the Round Table, Guinevere, Lancelot and the quest for the Holy Grail.' Arthur was a king ruling over a tribe. He lived in a castle in Camelot (probably South Camelot in Somerset) and fought the Saxons from c.470 to 500. His most famous victory was at Badon Hill. The monk Nennius wrote later that at his battle 'Arthur carried the cross of our Lord Jesus Christ on his shoulder for three days and nights and the Britons were victorious.' It is thought that Arthur died about 500 AD and is buried in Glastonbury Abbey. During later centuries many stories were told surrounding his fame. He had an illegitimate royal birth and was brought up by the magician Merlin. Merlin's activities would appear pure fairy story to children and were passed on in oral tradition from one

generation to another. Merlin made the Round Table for Arthur's twelve knights and is said to have built Stonehenge. He made sure that Arthur could draw the magic sword Excalibur out of a stone and that he met the beautiful Guinevere who became his queen. After their marriage, they settled in the West Country, but one of Arthur's knights, Lancelot, created 'the eternal triangle' by falling in love with Guinivere.

The *Sutton Hoo* ship found buried in East Anglia in 1939 probably contained the valuable belongings of an early Saxon king. No body has been found, but it is likely that the king was called Raedwald who died in 636. The articles found in the large ship included jewels, helmets, horns, glass beakers and other personal belongings. They are very valuable in themselves, as well as providing archaeological evidence for children to learn about Saxon boats and the articles owned by the wealthy. The British Museum houses them in a special gallery and publishes many useful pamphlets.

King Offa ruled Mercia (midlands and part of southern England) as a Saxon king during the late eighth century. He was 'a man of greater power, prestige and sophistication than his predecessors' (Wood, 1981) and left a strong, unified kingdom reaching to London and beyond. Offa was a typical authoritarian ruler supported by a strong army. He made his headquarters at Tamworth but in good weather travelled throughout his lands, going to London and hunting at Brentford. Although the Roman roads were by now difficult to use (because they had been built hundreds of years before and used a great deal) he travelled constantly. He and his followers ate large amounts of food – one night's eating included two oxen, ten geese, twenty hens, five salmon and ten eels. After taking control of Kent in 785 he became jealous of the Archbishop of Canterbury and created an archbishopric at Lichfield. He had his son consecrated as ruler of Mercia before he died to ensure the succession. He did not hesitate to murder the king of East Anglia who was in love with his daughter. His

Figure 4 'David playing a harp' – a painting made at Canterbury Cathedral by order of King Offa.

stone church in Brixworth is one of the earliest Anglo-Saxon buildings still standing today. Despite this, he is usually only remembered for his Dyke, built from the Severn estuary to the Irish Sea from 790 onwards, which fulfilled his desire to keep the Welsh out of Mercia. Slaves built over a hundred miles of a mound five feet deep with a wooden palisade at the top and forts and beacons to defend it. Parts of it still can be seen today, though less obviously than Hadrian's Wall. King Offa, therefore, not only built the Dyke

but was a very powerful ruler in an unruly age. The scholar Alcuin wrote of him 'Never forget Offa's fine Character, his modest way of life, his concern to reform the life of a Christian people, but do not follow him in his cruel and greedy acts' (Wood, 1981).

Saxon and British pagan gods and goddesses were replaced by crosses and later churches when Roman Christianity began to influence Britain. The story of the conversion to Christianity from St Augustine's visit to Kent in 590 to the Synod (church council) of Whitby in 664 embraces all parts of the British Isles. It is concerned with several outstanding 'saints' and many enthralling stories come from it. As early as 305 AD, Alban was martyred at St Albans; 'I am called Alban by my parents and I worship and adore the true and living God, who created all things' (Bede, 1990,). The original Celts had become Christians. Patrick went from Wales to Ireland to convert the Irish. One of his followers, Columba, sailed to Iona, an island on the west coast of Scotland, and set up a monastery still flourishing today. From Iona, Aidan crossed to the north of England (Northumbria) and set up another monastery at Lindisfarne. While these Celtic monks were setting up their own form of Christianity, Augustine arrived in Kent from Rome, converted King Ethelbert 'sitting in the open air' (Bede, 1990) and set up a Roman Christian church at Canterbury, now the cathedral. Celtic and Roman Christianity clashed when Paulinus, a monk in Augustine's following, converted King Edwin of Northumbria to Roman Christianity. One of Edwin's followers spoke of 'the present life of men . . . like the swift flight of a sparrow through the room, wherein you sit at supper in winter' (Bede, 1990). Northumbrian Christians became so confused by the different forms of Christianity that King Oswy called a synod at Whitby Abbey in 664. Here Abbess Hilda presided over the discussions. The differences between the hairstyles of monks (how much hair was shaven off), obedience to the Pope in Rome and the date of Easter were hotly debated. Roman rules were favoured in the end. Thus Northumbria led the way for Roman Catholic Christianity to be established.

During all these years, first wooden and then stone churches were built on the sites of many Celtic crosses as at Iona and Lindisfarne. Many young men and women were attracted to the religious life as an antidote to the warlike times of Offa and King Arthur. Monks from Europe brought learning from Europe (for example, Benedict Biscop). They were the only people to read and write. They wrote religious books by hand ('manuscripts', from the Latin word *manus* meaning 'hand') and started schools for boys in the monasteries. One of the most famous of these monks was a man called Bede. He spent most of his life at the monastery of Jarrow and wrote many learned books. In particular his *Ecclesiastical History of the English Nation* (up to his own death in 735) is still famous as the first history of England and provides us with clear evidence of events and people in the Saxon period, whether religious, political or social.

King Alfred of Wessex is usually termed 'a good king' in the terms of *1066 and All That* (Mandarin, 1991) though his biographer Bishop Asser has mainly been responsible for this view. Work on Alfred (849–899 AD) naturally divides itself into three large parts: Alfred's wars against the Vikings, his strengthening of Wessex for future attacks and his work for religion and learning. The ideas underlying a study of Alfred are easily understood by juniors. Many lively books suitable for children have been written. Marjorie Reeves' *Alfred and the Danes* ('Then and There' series, Longman, 1984) is excellent for teachers and more able pupil readers, and is a reasonably priced and scholarly account of his leadership of Wessex and defeat of Guthrum, the Viking leader. I strongly favour an in-depth study of Alfred, even though I have concentrated more on Arthur, Offa, the *Sutton Hoo* ship and the conversion of Britain to Christianity in the Anglo-Saxon period in this chapter.

Vikings

The Viking invasion and settlement of Britain has always been a popular topic in primary schools. They came from Norway, Sweden and Denmark, at first to plunder as they had poor land at home, then later, in Alfred's time, to settle. They attacked Lindisfarne monastery in Northumbria; *The Anglo-Saxon Chronicle* recounts under the date AD 793 'the harrowing inroads of heathen men made lamentable havoc in the church of God in

Holy Island, by rapine and slaughter'. They conquered East Anglia, Northumbria and Mercia, and only Alfred stood out against them in Wessex. They built magnificent rowing and sailing ships with carved prows and worshipped pagan gods such as Thor and Odin. Archaeologists have found many Viking objects in their archaeological digs, particularly in York. Although Alfred kept the Vikings at bay, after his death the Saxons were finally defeated and King Canute, from Denmark, became king of all England in 1016.

The content of what I have written here about core unit 1 – 'Romans, Anglo-Saxons and Vikings in Britain' – is mainly outline 'knowledge' with reference to less well known personalities. Until teachers can understand the period they are teaching and see it in the context of many parts and not as an isolated topic, they cannot convey to children of any age the true meaning of the past and its relevance to the present. This relevance and the ability to understand concepts, such as 'warrior king', 'sacrifice' and 'loyalty' in battle and the worship of pagan gods, are more important to children than the bare facts and certainly the bare dates. Teachers should constantly make comparison and contrast between the three different invaders and try to see how they link with each other. The content I have suggested on the Anglo-Saxons is more appropriate for Year 5 but may be selected from for Year 3. The Arthurian legends, the *Sutton Hoo* ship burial and King Alfred are suitable topics for Year 3.

Below, Russell Carter, Headmaster of Yaxley CE Junior School, Peterborough, describes his work on the Vikings with a Year 4 class of eight-year-olds.

The Vikings: A cross-curricular history-based topic for Year 4

For several years, Year 4 children have followed a term's history-based topic, 'The Vikings'. The National Curriculum has, therefore, brought little change. Following a short introduction on the Romans and the Saxons, during which the chronology of the period, shown on a large scale time-line, and a picture of what life was like in Britain prior to the Vikings is built up, we have continued to study that period in depth for most of the term.

The basis of our historical work has always been through the asking of *Historical Questions*, thus in our initial planning the selected questions are listed as *Key Issues*, using the grid given in 'G' of the Non-Statutory Guidance (1991). More detailed planning is then completed in fortnightly units using a grid with the following headings: Learning Objective (Key Issue/Question); Activities (Showing differentiation); Source Materials/Resources; Classroom Management; Level Description; Evidence/Bases of Attainment.

The key issues, on which the questions are posed, refer firstly to the background of the Vikings and their reasons for invading, then to them as sailors, raiders, settlers, farmers, traders and craftsmen. Through these, the political, economic, technological, scientific, social, religious, cultural and aesthetic perspectives are included. Each child is not expected to work on all of the issues but all will cover the introductory, 'Who were the Vikings?' and its supplementary questions, together with three or four of the others. Through differentiated groupwork, however, each issue is explored, and displays and presentations ensure that children are familiar with them all. To each issue, a very important question is added, 'How do we know?' Through this question children are led to the various historical sources from which most of the answers come. They are introduced to Viking sagas, stories, poems and proverbs, myths and legends and also the *Anglo-Saxon Chronicles*, from which local history is introduced through its many references to Peterborough. Replica artefacts, posters and reference books are available, the more recent ones containing copies of original sources.

However, many of the questions are answered through a visit to York, where, in 1993 the children spent three full days. There they not only saw evidence of the Vikings but also of the Romans and Saxons. Through visits to the Yorkshire Museum, the Jorvik Centre and the Archaeological Resource Centre (ARC) a real picture of the Vikings begins to emerge and the children learn of the importance of archaeological excavations and how they help to build up our knowledge. A day is spent in Houlgate Village, where the children dress and live as Vikings, building and repairing houses and other buildings, working as craftsmen in leather, wood or clay, tilling the ground as farmers, grinding the corn, keeping the houses clean and tidy or acting as the village guards looking out for Saxon raiders. A simple meal is provided and a Viking banquet is also available. As the visit is made in winter some of the disadvantages of Viking life are quickly discovered!

Back at school the questions continue to be explored as each issue is examined in as practical a way as possible. 'Excavations' are carried out in a corner of the school field, with the findings being carefully cleaned and catalogued as at Jorvik and the ARC. A life-sized Viking house has been designed and is under construction in another area of the field, to be completed next year. Within the classroom, longboats and sails are designed, made and tested, as are model houses and clothing such as helmets, shoes, dresses, as well as shields, swords and axes. Corn is ground into flour and made into bread, using an 'oven' built on the field and a simple potage is made and sampled. Wool straight from the school sheep is washed and dyed, using roots from the conservation area and then hand spun into yarns and woven into cloth. Plans have been drawn up for the construction of a replica loom, almost full-sized. Household utensils are made from clay, as well as more jewellery from leather and stones. A Viking board game, 'Hnefatafl', the forerunner of chess, is made and played. Research into Viking trade routes and navigation across the North Sea, into Europe and across the Atlantic is carried out, as

are investigations into the legacy of Viking place names and words left in our language. Runes (Viking letters of the alphabet) are made and used, simulations of the planning of Viking raids and the setting up of settlements are carried out through computer programs. Much of this is carried further through drama, as are sagas, myths and legends, as well as modern stories of the Vikings. Thus the topic is truly cross-curricular, with contributions from geography, science, art, technology as well as English.

However, it is the historical content which is the most important aspect, and the major events and personalities of the period are researched and details added to the class time-line in the process. Through the topic children are able to see how British society was shaped by the invaders and to understand many historical concepts such as cause and consequence. It also fosters the ability to understand and analyse different interpretations and points of view and to use resources and make their own judgements based on evidence. As seen in the planning grid, the teachers make ongoing assessments of each child's progress and many of the tasks provided are set with this in mind. The assessment might be through question and answer, observation, the product of the task or an extra task set solely for the purpose. However the topic is planned and carried out, there are no shortages of opportunity for assessment.

The topic concluded with a parents' evening, where the children dressed up in Viking costume and treated the adults to a 'banquet' with food, demonstrations and entertainment made and served by themselves. A video of the visit to York was also shown.

As well as Core unit 1, the topic covers not only an element of our local history unit, but also the first section of two Extension studies, 'Ships and seafarers' and 'Domestic life, families and childhood', continued in future history topics. 'Food and farming' could also be covered in this way.

LIFE IN TUDOR TIMES (KEY STAGE 2: CORE UNIT 2)

This is a colourful period in English history, and it is good news that this unit is compulsory. It is full of interesting content but can also be a trap for unsuspecting teachers, as many of the concepts involved are foreign to the twentieth century. For instance, the concepts listed in Diagram 10 of the Non-Statutory Guidance (1991) (e.g. court, patron, belief, law) are mostly unfamiliar to primary children and will all need explaining. Out of seventeen concepts only three may already be understood (trade, industry, and scientific discoveries). An awareness of Tudor 'ways of thinking' is needed for teachers to make the facts historical and interesting. This can only come with reading, thinking and discussion on the part of teachers and children. The following section is intended to help teachers become 'aware' of the period.

The unit appears rather vague. How are we to decide what 'major events' means? 'Way of life' is also an imprecise term. 'Major events' and 'personalities' require teachers to be familiar with the secondary and primary sources for the period. The palaeography (handwriting) in written documents from this period needs learning, although transcripts are usually available from record offices which have, in the past, been happy to help teachers. The proliferation of glittering and unique Tudor personalities presents too much choice. Should we select the old favourites such as Sir Francis Drake and Sir Walter Raleigh, or dare to investigate less familiar figures such as Sir Christopher Hatton, John Gerard and Sir Humphrey Gilbert? How do we get to know about them easily and quickly? Remember, also, that Wales, Scotland and Ireland should be considered, specially since the Tudor century left

such a permanent mark on all three. Although listed as an 'event' in the 1994 Dearing Proposals, the 'break with Rome' is a difficult concept to grasp fully, as are all 'religious changes', because it happened over a long period of time and is therefore hardly an event. Henry VIII's negotiations with the Pope were long and difficult and the 'break' came about over many years, culminating in Acts of Parliament and followed by the gradual dissolution of the monasteries.

Too many 'goodies' means we have to select ruthlessly. I am limiting my selection to some monarchs and their courts, some events, some ways of life and certain other personalities. These events are of national importance and as the figures are from the upper class, they are well documented.

Which Monarchs?

Unlike core units 3 and 4 ('Victorian Britain' and 'Britain since 1930'), the monarchs in the Tudor period are powerful people with the ability to promote and bestow material rewards and finally to kill (note that Henry VIII executed two of his six wives and 'put one away'). In the Tudor period, the position of the monarch was crucially linked with the religious upheaval between Roman Catholics and Protestants on the continent and the widespread fear of a Roman Catholic monarch from France or Spain. Selection of monarchs for me depends upon their representing these crucial themes and upon the availability of suitable sources, both pictorial and written. Therefore I would select Henry VIII and Elizabeth I.

Henry VIII

Henry VIII represents Tudor domination after weak medieval monarchy and the stability of his father's reign. This domination was to last until 1649 – the execution of Charles I. So we associate with Henry VIII: power, wealth, extravagence and take-over of the monasteries but also failure in marriage (six wives and no stable succession) and loss of his ship the *Mary Rose* (named after his favourite sister). Holbein's portraits represent his strength and power whether they are accurate or not!

Elizabeth I

Henry VIII's daughter, Elizabeth I, who according to her own words had 'the body of a weak and feeble woman, but the heart and stomach of a king, and a king of England too', also represents Tudor domination but in a more personal form. In spite of her father's fear for England under a woman ruler, her sex gave her power over a masculine court. Her reign was a long one (forty-five years) and teachers should emphasise her desire to remain unmarried and independently powerful, the splendour of her court and famous courtiers, the execution of Mary Stuart and the Armada fiasco.

Which events are important historically and understandable and colourful to juniors?

A time-line is essential for the purpose of clarifying the most important events. Put your selected events (and only those) on to your time-line. Some events are important historically; for example the fall of Cardinal Wolsey, the execution of Mary Stuart, and the Armada. Some events are colourful and understandable, such as the Battle of Flodden Field and the sinking of the *Mary Rose*. Some are both, and those are the ones to select. For me, these would include the Battle of Bosworth Field, the break with Rome, and the

Armada. These topics are well resourced in many ways, but there are intricacies to be understood. Recent celebrations in 1988 of the 1588 Armada show that England did not *defeat* Spain in battle: the conflict continued at sea until James I made peace with Spain in 1604. Spanish historians have expressed a very different point of view. So there is plenty of opportunity to use sources and put them up against each other to show different points of view. As suggested in the 1994 Proposals, 'exploitation overseas' may be exemplified by Drake's voyage round the world: I would use Richard Hakluyt's *Voyages* as source material here.

Figure 5   Miniature portrait of an *Unknown Young Man* by Nicholas Hilliard (1572)

Figure 6   Ancient view of Scarborough 1538 (attributed to 1485)

Ways of life

'Ways of life' of all social classes in town and country is a tall order, even for history specialists. It is useful to see how the publishers have wrestled with it in a limited number of words. All authors have realised that the conventional divisions into town and country, rich and poor and workers and leisured is too vague. This may seem a topic suitable for juniors but 'how people lived' is complicated and sophisticated historically. It would be difficult to study in our own age;

'people' can mean at least six categories. Traditions die hard and people's way of life and thought (in contrast to the Fire of London or a battle) are slow to change. This is best treated locally so that children can visit buildings and find out about local people from inventories and books in their own libraries and record offices (see Robert Guyver's work). So it is a good opportunity to link with Extension study B, a study of local history. For example, Chester, still with walls and old houses, had tremendous growth and prosperity in these centuries. Many of the black and white half-timbered houses can still be visited. But all over the country in this period there were these houses and others such as the Great Houses of Hardwick Hall, Hatfield House and Hampton Court Palace, as well as very small cottages (not now evident).

Social class remained hierarchical throughout the period and was never questioned, 'status' according to birth was taken for granted. 'Rising from the dust', in the words of Henry VII, was usual, and ambition was considered 'a good thing' even if it meant killing or ruining another man/woman. There are well-documented examples of this. Henry VII's tax collectors, Richard Empson and Edmund Dudley, were not only hated as tax collectors (compare our Inland Revenue) but because they were hard-working, ambitious 'middle-class' men, keen to please the king at the expense of wealthy aristocrats whom they had always envied. Henry VIII killed them in 1509! Bess of Hardwick started life as a ladies' maid from a poor farmer's home, married wealthy men four times, inheriting their money, built Hardwick Hall on her own design and was grandmother to Lady Arabella Stuart who had a claim to the English throne on Elizabeth I's death. Raleigh, Drake and Shakespeare all started life as poor men and rose through their own abilities and good fortune. Merchant craftsmen became wealthy men if their work was good. Robert Brerewood, a glover of Chester, was said to be as wealthy as London glovemakers. He became mayor of Chester and the townspeople built him an impressive house! Yet only aristocrats had any control over government and got close to the monarch.

'Rogues and vagabonds' were taken for granted and the 1601 Poor Law made parishes look after their own poor, thus saving the crown responsibility and expense. Life in the street was dangerous and 'gentlemen' walked on the gutter side of the street and wore a sword on their left side to draw it to defend their lady from 'gutter-snipes'. This area of the unit can become 'grey', therefore local examples of people, buildings and places must be used to give specific detail. Interesting and well-documented topics are big houses (local houses, food, architecture, Elizabeth I's 'progresses' around the south-east of the country); craftsmen and apprentices (guilds and mystery plays – here a link with drama); travel (barges on the River Thames, horses, coaches, sailing ships, roads, highwayman); and the poor in town and country. Though not as well resourced, the lives of children in this period is a relevant topic. The main emphasis for 'ways of life' should be on the stark contrasts between rich and poor; and lack of mobility for most people (and therefore news); the lack of really old people (Elizabeth I died at the amazingly old age of sixty-eight); the intense religious fervour (whether Anglican, Roman Catholic or Puritan); and personal loyalty. These characteristics should

Figure 7 A Seventeenth-century schoolboy by W. Theed, (monument to Sir Humphrey Chetham, Manchester Cathedral)

be compared or contrasted with ways of life in the 1990s. Much discussion is needed here, as facts do not speak for themselves in this period of the past.

The vitality and exuberance of this period, in spite of poverty, disease and early death, is exemplified by a host of interesting personalities who appeal to many primary children. Mary Queen of Scots (Mary Stuart) is not named in this Tudor study unit, though she is indicated for a study in depth in Extension study D. In fact the religious turmoil of the Tudor period can be summarized in explaining her life in France, Scotland and England up to her execution in 1587 in England. She may seem a romantic figure but all her marriages were failures; she was a very sad character and a victim of cruel circumstances. There were other vital people too. Sir Christopher Hatton, one of Elizabeth's courtiers (always in love with her but a bachelor all his life) showed the fine outstanding abilities of many of those whom the queen gathered around her.

Robert Guyver, a member of the 1989 History Working Group compiled two teachers' packs on *Tudor and Stuart Times*. In the following account he relates some important Tudor themes to the local history of Essex.

Selected Tudor themes illustrated from Essex history

Henry VIII's break with Rome

John Payne was a priest who was also steward to a well-known and powerful Essex family – the Petres of Ingatestone Hall. Sir William Petre had been a 'visitor' of religious houses in 1539 and on March 1 of that year had been instrumental in closing down Plymouth Priory. He was Secretary to four successive monarchs – Henry VIII, Edward VI, Mary I and Elizabeth I – and he accumulated enough wealth to buy land at Ingatestone which had once been part of the estate of Barking Abbey. Some years after the death of Sir William, John Payne was arrested (in 1581) and hanged the following year in Chelmsford market place.

William Shakespeare

Shakespeare is not necessarily easy to resource. I thought of using extracts from *Lamb's Tales from Shakespeare*, but decided to provide a link through the story of the ex-actor Will Kemp who was sacked by Shakespeare for adding to the original text and telling jokes. Will Kemp was the Michael Palin of his day – a witty and entertaining publicity-seeker. He morris danced from London to Norwich through Essex. In the Essex Record Office is a complaint to the Quarter Sessions which Kemp made about the state of the (Roman) road between Chelmsford and Braintree in 1599. 'This foul way I could find no ease in; thick woods being on either side, likewise being full of deep potholes, sometimes I skipped up to the waist.' Autolycus in *The Winter's Tale* (1611) (Scene IV, ii 30) sings: 'Jog on, jog on, the foot-path way, And merrily hent the stile-a: A merry heart goes all the day. Your sad tires in a mile-a.' Was Shakespeare thinking of his former employee?

The British Empire

Stories of the beginning of the British Empire are not easy to link with Essex until I realised that many earlier settlers in North America came from Essex. The Governor of *The Mayflower*, Christopher Martin, came from Great Burstead in Essex, and the captain, Christopher Jones, from Harwich. His house can still be seen. It was from Harwich in 1578 that Martin Frobisher set sail to the frozen wastes of North Canada returning only with fools' gold.

VICTORIAN BRITAIN (KEY STAGE 2: CORE UNIT 3)

In many schools, children think that 'the past' starts in 1837, the accession of Queen Victoria. Before the National Curriculum, the Victorian period was well taught and learnt as part of topic work. Children repeatedly studied that age because it is so prolific in excellent accessible sources such as artefacts, documents, buildings, photographs and even oral history through the memory of octogenarians. Thus it is now necessary to give teachers 'a new look' about the Victorian age. The unit has necessarily been selective and has omitted all the political and military excitement of the resignation of Sir Robert Peel over the Corn Laws, the premierships of Disraeli and Gladstone and the Boer Wars. The unit concentrates on how all types of people lived and worked, particularly as a result of industralialisation, beginning in the previous century. As class divisions from beggar to royalty were clearly defined and most people expected to remain in the station to which they were born, much work is involved in studying life in all these areas. This gives an opportunity for local examples and sources to be used, linking onto Extension study B, a study of local history.

The opportunity is given in the National Curriculum to study some topics in depth as long as all are covered to some extent, possibly using a time-line from 1837 to 1901. Even this is a demanding exercise in one term or more. Therefore, selection of suitable topics depends upon the interests of the teacher and the resources available. As Jo Lawrie and Paul Noble (1990) wrote in their excellent guide *Victorian Times* '. . . the legacies of the Victorian age are all around us, both in our buildings and in our institutions'. Children at school in big cities such as London, Manchester and Leeds have not far to look for large artefacts. Country areas also have farm buildings and cottages left, even if they have been altered. Above all, nearly all children still have railway lines, if not stations and trains to see. I have selected seven topics which interest me and

which would be understood by primary children, but teachers may want to select fewer than seven. My chosen topics would include: Queen Victoria, child labour, education, transport, towns, buildings and the place of women in society. I shall illustrate these from local examples familiar to me, as all teachers should.

Queen Victoria

When asked what 'Victorian' meant, a child answered 'it is something to do with Victoria Station'! It is good to see Queen Victoria named specifically in the new unit as the exemplar of 'The Victorian family'. The topic of the Queen, who reigned from 1837 to 1901 (sixty-four years), is a particularly attractive one for juniors and is hardly out of place in a study of Victorian Britain. Her name is given to many buildings, roads, parks and books, as well as a point of view! Although a 'constitutional limited monarch' she had considerable influence over politicians and policy, as did her husband Prince Albert until his untimely death in 1864. Like Elizabeth I, she has got the reputation of being a very successful ruler in spite of only being eighteen on her accession; Elizabeth I was twenty-five. If unit 2 has already been studied, it would be interesting to ask children in what way they were successful rulers. The relationship of Victoria to Elizabeth II may be seen on a family tree. Here Victoria's connection with Germany is clear, as are also the marriages to foreign princes of many members of the royal family until George VI and the present Prince of Wales. Victoria represents the perfect mother of nine children as an example to all other Victorian mothers. She adored her husband, though it was a politically arranged marriage, and had a very happy family life, though she would have preferred not to have had so many children. There is plenty of reliable source material for this family life from the queen's private letters as well as biographers. In her diary for 20 June, 1837 Victoria, aged eighteen, wrote:

> 'I was awoke at 6 o'clock by Mamma who told me the Archbishop of Canterbury and Lord Chamberlain wished to see me. I got out of bed and went into my sitting-room (only in my dressing-gown) and *alone* . . . The Lord Chamberlain then acquainted me that my poor uncle, the King, was no more, and had expired twelve minutes past two this morning, and consequently that I am *Queen*' (*Queen Victoria's Diaries 1832–40*, John Murray, 1912).

Her life at Osborne House on the Isle of Wight has been particularly well documented. This house was the creation of Victoria and Albert and descriptions of family life there show Victoria to have been a lively and active parent. She had art lessons, and her sketches and paintings of her children at Osborne are fascinating historical sources. Victoria and Albert also bought and improved the Balmoral estate and spent August there in her Scottish realm each year. Elizabeth II and her family still keep up this tradition. References to Osborne lead to the popularity of seaside resorts for health reasons, made easier by the railway boom when places such as Brighton, Scarborough and Blackpool were at their heyday. This established the summer 'seaside holiday' popular in the country until the start of World War II.

Victoria's upper-class social life links on to costume both in her class of society and in other classes. The speed of the new sewing machine enabled wealthy people to have more clothes made by 'the dressmaker', though mass production of cheaper clothes and mail order came in the later part of the period. Male and female clothes were heavy, formal and very elaborate. Women wore very full skirts over crinolines and bustles, and men wore dark suits, starched collars and waistcoats. Children wore the miniature fashions of their parents, as in earlier centuries. Poorer people and servants had informal clothes more like our clothes today. The

Figure 8 Queen Victoria as a young woman, by William Fowler

layers of clothing worn were largely the result of colder houses. Costume may be linked with leisure activities and entertainment, including music halls, circuses and street entertainments, such as watching monkeys on barrel organs.

Child labour

Poor children made a striking contrast to the royal children. 'Child labour' is important in the unit, and this leads to the big topic of industrialisation, factories, mines, chimney-sweeps and bad housing conditions. Specific local examples will give the topic more life, for example apprentices working in Samuel Greg's mill at Quarry Bank, Styal, Cheshire, (National Trust). Good factory owners treated their apprentices well in comparison with the conditions and attitudes in the new city factories. The ills of poor children are well depicted in Charles Dickens' *David Copperfield* and *Oliver*

Twist, Charles Kingsley's *The Water Babies* and Frances Trollope's *Michael Armstrong*. Teachers could select extracts from these, as well as Mrs Gaskell's *Mary Barton* about Manchester factory workers. Such children did not go to school and died young. Richard Oastler and Lord Shaftesbury helped to improve their lot by factory reports and acts of Parliament. The books mentioned above are valuable as written contemporary sources of the period, though many modern books for children are useful as present-day views of the past.

Education

A natural step from this topic on children is their schooling. This is an ever-popular and successful topic with plenty of suitable resources and examples for easy role-playing and dressing-up. (See the account of *Sevington School* in Chapter 9.) But it can become monotonous if too much time is spent on it in too many years of schooling. Children need to enlarge their horizons and to learn more about Victorian Britain than schooling. Bring a new dimension to the study of children by using more well-known literature; for example, Lewis Carroll's *Alice in Wonderland* is contemporary fiction but also highly imaginative and amusing. It depicts the interests of Victorian children in fairy stories. Another example might be Charles Dicken's *Nicholas Nickleby* showing life in a badly run 'private' school. It is possible to use parts of these as actual sources and also to role-play some of the scenes. Dr Barnardo, founder of

THE COTTON FAMINE: GROUP OF MILL OPERATIVES AT MANCHESTER.—SEE PAGE 558.

Figure 9   The cotton famine: a group of mill operatives at Manchester (1862)

the famous 'Homes' for children, is also worthy of detailed consideration.

Transport

No study of Victorian Britain is complete without an understanding of the vast changes in people's lives by improved transport. The most influential development was that of the railways. Huge steam locomotives, found in museums, are a source of the Victorian period in themselves. Other engineering feats were breathtaking experiences for Victorians; the Olive Mount cutting at Liverpool, the carriages of the Liverpool Manchester Railway and the huge elaborate station buildings (e.g. St Pancras, Shrewsbury and Brighton) are only some of these artefacts still to be seen. There are plenty of resources to use including the 'Railway Time Tables' started by George Bradshaw of Pendleton, Salford. Railways not only carried people more quickly than horses

or coaches but they also made much more money by carrying coal and manufactured goods from the new industries developed during the century.

Bicycles, steamships and the first cars are also part of this topic on transport. Railways are linked to quicker transport of letters and the Penny Post, so leading to better communications around the country. This topic has close links with the extension of railway lines and stations all over the country. By 1860 the railway revolution was truly accomplished.

Towns

With the exception of London, towns grew into cities in the Victorian period mainly because of industrialisation. Large numbers of people were needed to work in the new factories, so poor farm-workers went into towns. Small 'back to back' houses were built near the factories so that

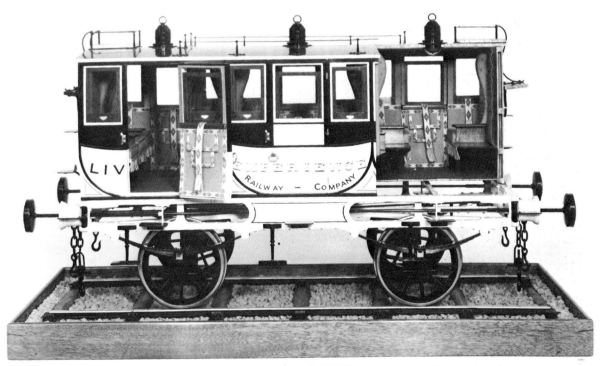

Figure 10 Liverpool to Manchester railway: a first-class coach (1834)

workers could be at their work early in the morning. The population increased in these areas, and slums developed with the attendant disease and death. Areas of the north-west, Teeside, South Wales, Birmingham and Glasgow saw the greatest growth. There was no town planning and only thoughtful employers built comfortable houses around their factories. This was really only possible in country areas; Sir Titus Salt built such a community at Saltaire near Bradford and his factory village is still standing today. Manchester experienced great growth in factories and population, and Queen Victoria conferred the status of 'city' on the town in 1853. The Manchester Ship Canal was built in the late 1880s and took goods to the port of Liverpool. This was an engineering feat which made Manchester more prosperous. The increasingly wealthy middle classes built areas and streets of 'substantial' town houses until they moved out to the 'suburbs', and often owned houses in the country as well. At the other social extreme were the slum dwellings. Families lived in one or two rooms with water collected from a pump in the street and no sewage system. Death among children was very common. Dickens' Oliver Twist learnt to become a thief in order to survive. The difference between the wealth of the industrialists and the poverty of their employees stirred the hearts of many social reformers such as Dr Barnardo (children), Dr Kay (schools) and Edwin Chadwick (health); they started 'voluntary' organisations and persuaded Parliament to pass acts to help poorer people.

Buildings

Much good and evil came from the new industrial cities, including smoke from the factories; but one unmitigated success was magnificent municipal buildings. These included many town halls, such as Manchester Town Hall erected between 1864 and 1874, unequalled in Europe. Concert halls, art galleries, law courts, libraries, the new 'civic' universities and railway stations were also built in Gothic style. The Victoria and Albert Museum in London is an obvious example. These large artefacts provide plenty of evidence for children to use in their study of Victorian Britain.

Cameras were invented about 1840, and old photographs are an excellent source of evidence for all primary children. City life encouraged the size and number of newspapers, particularly in the early evening to catch city-dwellers returning home from work. Many Victorian editions of newspapers are in libraries and form good contemporary evidence for children's work.

Women in society

The position of upper-class women began to alter during this period, leading to the Suffragette Movement for women's votes in the next reign. Well-documented women include Queen Victoria, Florence Nightingale and Mary Seacole. This period presents a good opportunity to consider gender issues emanating from men's attitudes towards women and women's necessary acceptance of this view of inferiority, mainly for economic reasons. Not only were working-class women used in factories and mines, for example as matchmakers at the Bryant and May factory, and as domestic servants, but middle-class and upper-class women were expected to marry and produce large families regardless of their own inclinations. Very few girls were allowed to receive higher education or even schooling. Mrs Beaton's *Book of Household Management* was a popular manual for middle-class women, making 'household management' into an unpaid job. Academic schools were founded by Misses Buss and Beale, Emily Davies founded Girton College, Cambridge, and women slowly began to enter the professions. At the same time, match girls at Bryant and May went on strike for better wages. Many women became writers as the only opening for their talents; Mrs Gaskell, the Brontë sisters, Elizabeth Barrett Browning and George Eliot are the most famous.

The Great Exhibition of 1851

The Great Exhibition of 1851 was the brain-child of Prince Albert. This was an exhibition of goods from all over the world in a specially constructed glass building in Hyde Park. One of its purposes was to show how advanced Britain was industrially and to encourage other countries to buy her goods. After the exhibition closed, the whole building was moved to Sydenham and called the Crystal Palace. A great profit was made from visitors to the exhibition and this was used to buy the sites for the present South Kensington Museums.

Teachers may find it difficult to introduce the Victorian period in Wales, Scotland and Ireland, except incidentally unless more time than a term is spent on the topic or some of the suggested themes are omitted. The Irish Potato Famine of 1846 and the beginning of increasing emigration of poor Irish people to England has introduced a more cosmopolitan social life to Britain. The period is a good one to study because of its ebullience, the material evidence and stark contrasts between the rich and the poor, and the obvious legacy it has left to children in the late-twentieth century.

BRITAIN SINCE 1930 (KEY STAGE 2: CORE UNIT 4)

If understanding chronology is one of the aims of the National Curriculum in History, the break between the end of unit 3 in 1901 and 1930 is more surprising than the omission of the eighteenth century. More so, as the Edwardian period (1901–10) is well defined in British history with plenty of resources suitable for juniors. A time-line from 1837 to 1994 is therefore very important as a start to understanding this omission. It is as well to omit the Great War (1914–18) as confusion might arise with World War II which is so much more relevant to today's children. The Great War is studied in Key Stage 3. The advantages of unit 4 are the links that can be made between the 1930s and the present day, the oral evidence available from living persons, the photographs (*Picture Post* magazine from 1938), the film resources, as well as written evidence in which there are few language difficulties. During this period it is important to help children to appreciate what vast changes have taken place in just three generations. In future years junior children should be able to build upon their Key Stage 1 experience of studying the twentieth century in family history. Difficulties arise for

teachers who are too close to the events to interpret fairly what happened beyond their own small environment. One point of view may unconsciously be given of an event or personality. Another difficulty, at present, is a lack of suitable reading books for older juniors, though class pupils' books are rapidly being published in series for the National Curriculum. At teacher level, there are biographies of important people, but so far little that is well illustrated and lively in style. Perhaps this is a reason for studying this unit in Years 3 and 4, and leaving units 1 and 2 for the older junior year. Yorkshire Television comes to the rescue with the famous and well-used series *How we used to live*, accompanied by the popular *Time Line* and *Family Pack* for the twentieth century from Pictorial Charts Educational Trust. But this unit 4 does lend itself to the use of local examples and oral history.

Themes to be developed in detail are endless, and I am only suggesting those I find most interesting, from which teachers should again select. These include the 1930s as a decade, World War II and Winston Churchill, the post-war Welfare State, the position of women and immigrants, the Green Movement, leisure and entertainment, changes in transport, the technological revolution and architectural issues.

The 1930s

During the 1930s the English class system separated most members of society, the media was not all-pervading and there were widely different ways of life. The Jarrow March of 1936 led by Ellen Wilkinson, a Labour MP, represented the dire position of the unemployed; Jarrow was a ship-building town where 68 per cent of workers were unemployed. Nationally, this poverty lifted towards the end of the decade as the armament industry revived and the fears of war began to be felt. Therefore it was a decade of anxiety for many. It was hardly surprising that material conditions should be uppermost in most people's lives. Meanwhile, there were those who were somewhat 'better off ' and could afford to buy their own houses, which in turn led to more house-building and 'ribbon development' of private houses along roads into towns. People

became interested in home comforts and entertainment, such as gramophones, radios (wirelesses), vacuum cleaners and refrigerators. The cinema had a boom period, and many people went to watch a black and white 'silent' film, or later a 'talkie', on a Friday night – a night out for a couple instead of men going to the pub alone. Odeon cinemas in huge American-style buildings could be found in most large urban centres. They had a restaurant, dance halls and sometimes organs rising from the basement which played popular jazz tunes. Reginald Dixon made Blackpool famous as an organist. He rose up from the basement with his organ, wearing full evening dress amidst loud clapping from the audience. More people owned cheap Austin, Ford or Morris cars; bicycles and 'sidecars' were popular and 'charabancs' took holiday-makers to Britain's holiday camps as well as on day trips to country places. On account of the depression many people limited their number of children – 'the baby Austin ousted the baby. The nursery gave place to the garage', in the words of the historian A. J. P. Taylor (1965).

Figure 11   The drawing room of Mr Straw's house in Worksop (1932)

THE DAUGHTER WHO HEAPED ON THE *COAL*

SAVE FUEL FOR BATTLE

ISSUED BY THE MINISTRY OF FUEL AND POWER

Figure 12 'Save fuel for battle', a Second World War poster issued by the Ministry of Fuel and Power

Word War II and Winston Churchill

World War II is already used as a very stimulating topic in this period. There are many very good resources and teachers can usually find their own fairly easily from parents and grandparents. It also introduced Winston Churchill at the height of his power; he is perhaps to date the only outstanding personality since 1930 who can be understood by primary children. The war had a tremendous social impact on Britain; the lives of young people between the ages of eighteen and thirty were completely altered, there was acute disruption of social life, many were killed and maimed and material conditions turned upside down. Apart from victory over the Axis powers which removed that menace, the only benefits were the unity of the classes, the courage forced upon many and

the desire to build a more just society after the war. The obvious themes for junior children include the evacuations of city school children in 1939 and 1940 (47 per cent of all children), the blitz of 1940–1 especially affecting London (over fifteen thousand killed there), Birmingham, Sheffield, Coventry and Liverpool, as well as southern ports.

Home owners provided 'Anderson' shelters in gardens and 'Morrison' shelters indoors to shelter from air-raids. All comers in London and Liverpool used underground station platforms to sleep in at night. Gas masks, black-out curtains, food, fuel and clothes rationing, fire-watching (in the new 'siren' suits) and dimmed headlights were attendant features of the 'war effort'. Railways, still the main means of transporting goods, arms and troops, were constantly disruptedby air-raids. Evacuation brought to light the difficult home conditions of many city children. There was full employment, including women and girls; factories producing war weapons worked long hours. Morale was boosted by Vera Lynn singing to the troops, and radio programmes such as *ITMA* (*It's That Man Again*) with its hero Tommy Handley. Young people in the many branches of the armed forces were the only people to experience any sort of social life; some of those 'had a good war', if not killed or maimed in active service. When the Americans joined in the war after Pearl Harbour and their troops came over to Britain, many girls became 'GI brides'. Most people grew their own food, and allotments and back gardens became very productive. Michael Foreman (1989) has written an engaging book for juniors *War Boy* depicting his country childhood during the war. It is beautifully illustrated by the author and is a true history of the war from a child's point of view.

The post-war Welfare State

Two far-reaching consequences of the war were thought out in the hope that Hitler would be defeated and Britain would need better social

Figure 13 A prefabricated house (1951)

conditions. Sir William Beveridge wrote the Beveridge Report in 1942 to persuade Parliament to introduce personal insurance and health care for all people. Rab Butler, a Conservative politician, thought out the Education Act of 1944 to give all children free primary and secondary education. Thus the six years of World War II altered many people's lives at the time and gave greater social security from 1945 onwards.

Implementing the 'Welfare State' became the main job of the Labour Government of 1945. The material rebuilding of the country took until 1955, as houses were in extremely short supply and the post-war baby boom led to very great shortages of accommodation. Unemployment benefit, holidays with pay and the many employment openings after the war led to a healthier and better-housed population.

The position of women and immigrants

The part played by most young women in the war, particularly in dangerous occupations, gradually led to more job opportunities for women, though in the early years of 1945 to 1955 men were still favoured as returning 'saviours of the nation' in jobs traditionally held by men. This particularly applied to the heavy engineering industries and bus driving and conducting, in which women had replaced men during the war. The 1975 Equal Opportunities Act officially aimed to give women more opportunities in the market place and great strides have been made since then. But recent examples have shown that, although women can be employed and have a 'job', they are still not able to reach the top, and come up against what is called 'a glass ceiling' in many areas of work. Married women have earned maternity leave since the 1950s, but this is uneven in its implementation and there is still inadequate provision in child care for children up to five years of age, so jettisoning chances of promotion for women. Therefore 'the way of life' of women (half the population) has improved since the 1930s but not enough.

The same applies to the old and new immigrants to Britain from different parts of the world, particularly refugees from Hitler's Europe and arrivals from former members of the British Empire and present members of the

Commonwealth. The European immigrants, particularly, included distinguished people who enriched British intellectual life. Workers from other continents were encouraged to come to Britain to undertake low-paid jobs. Many were intelligent and hard working and started their own businesses. These flourished and many held influential positions in the community, such as the Pakistani Lord Mayor of Bradford. But advancement in the professions has been even slower than that of women, and immigrants are still discriminated against in their homes and workplaces. Emigration to parts of the Commonwealth has not been as great since 1945 as it was in the nineteenth century, but many parts of Canada, Australia, New Zealand and Southern Africa are worked in by British men and women who could not find a satisfying life in post-war Britain.

The Green Movement

The environmental health of the country has improved from the point of view of air pollution which was once caused by fogs combining with the soot from smoking chimneys. This improvement occured with the wider use of oil, electricity and gas for heating and domestic use. But the Green Movement has shown that the disposal of nuclear waste and other hazards which are, on the surface, economical solutions, may become more and more dangerous to the environment. Many junior schools are involved in saving the environment through the collection of paper, glass, clothing and metals which can be recycled.

Leisure and entertainment

With shorter hours of work, people had more time for leisure and entertainment, which have become money-making businesses. Ballroom dancing and the cinema gave way to television

and jazz, and then rock groups provided entertainment from the 1960s to the present. Cinemas only survived if the 'big screen' was used and productions such as *South Pacific* and *The Sound of Music* were screened. The 'swinging sixties' introduced teenage fashion as an art in itself and young people became more independent from their parents. Football became a national obsession and big money was to be made from it. The influence of traditional religion and the social life of the church were having less effect on youth. The media generally, especially newspapers, strongly influenced public opinion from the 1960s onwards and could ruin careers by true or false allegations, leading to libel cases and more work for lawyers. Children's fiction, detective stories and magazines have all increased and provide another form of entertainment. Packaged holidays became popular, and in the 1970s people ventured to the Mediterranean to find the sun. British holiday resorts became deserted as they cost more than holidays abroad.

These aspects are worth mentioning, but it would be a great pity if teachers allowed an in-depth study of famous football players or a jazz favourite to be considered as a piece of serious historical work, unless the study was related to social background, and change, continuity and time were linked to it. The sources used would tend to be newspaper cuttings and booklets from the club concerned, rather than books.

Changes in transport

The enjoyment of these broader and more intense leisure pursuits were facilitated by better transport by road and air, though not by rail. The building of Spaghetti Junction, joining eighteen roads in the Birmingham area, represents the scale of change. The 'baby Austin' of the 1930s has been superseded by larger and more powerful cars, and more people drive, with the car becoming another symbol of material prosperity.

Air travel gradually became cheaper from the 1970s onwards and competition arose between different airlines resulting in cheaper package holidays. The helicopter also became a useful form of transport for short distances, especially for sea and mountain rescues. The Channel Tunnel, started in 1990, is intended to be a quick route to Europe for trains and cars, another form of speedier communications. How far these better communications improve the quality of life has yet to be seen, but they have increased the speed and range of social life, broadened outlooks of many types of people and have also made everybody less dependent upon family life.

The technological revolution

The revolution in high technology began in the 1970s, though many inventions were proving labour-saving devices in the home before that decade. In addition to television and radio, most households now have vacuum cleaners, washing machines, refrigerators and freezers, tumble-driers, dishwashers, microwaves and cake/food mixers as well as central heating. Launderettes are used by those without their own washing machines or driers. Sir Clive Sinclair invented many new ideas, some of which became popular – pocket calculators, cheap computers, digital watches and the electric car. Car telephones are used for business and personal purposes. Medical advances from the 1940s onwards were helped by technology – penicillin (discovered in 1928) and other antibiotics, injections against many diseases (for example, polio), safer and faster surgical operations, better pain-killing drugs and body scanners. Viruses have replaced infectious

diseases as the greatest threat to public health. All these inventions have not only made life easier, but have prolonged it, thus making for an older, but fitter population. In some ways they have led to isolation and lack of support for the smaller family.

Architectural issues

Some of the following topics will appear mundane and obvious to the older teacher, but in comparison with other units in the National Curriculum they have a tremendous effect on all classes of society today and therefore form obvious links with children's lives which soon become part of twentieth-century history. All around us we see architecture from the 1930s, and historical visits are easier to plan than in core units 1, 2 and 3. There is no need for long journeys to the Jorvic Centre at York to seek out signs of the Vikings or to Hampton Court Palace to view Cardinal Wolsey's memorial in brick. The following buildings should not be dismissed as 'not history': 1930s semi-detached houses, prefabricated war and post-war accommodation, 1960s high-rise flats (if not already destroyed), concrete shopping precincts, Odeon cinemas and some of the more artistic buildings such as the art deco Hoover factory in West London (now a new Tesco store). Prince Charles' predelictions about new architecture compared with old should be discussed and an effort made to see changes in the built environment. Children should learn to observe the buildings around them and the houses they live in as part of history. An in-depth study of the development/change of styles of architecture since 1930 would be well worth while.

ANCIENT GREECE (KEY STAGE 2: CORE UNIT 5)

The civilisation of Ancient Greece and the legacy it has given to us in the modern world is the main emphasis of this core unit. The focus is upon

Greek ways of life, beliefs and successes. 'Civilisation' is a sophisticated word for primary children. It can mean a multitude of things –

buildings, art, drama, writings, thought and language, and in this case, sporting achievement. The focus suggests ways of getting to know about this 'civilisation'. Teachers' views vary as to when this should be studied in the junior school. The length of the period, about four thousand years, and complexity of concepts and names point to Years 5 and 6, though Russell Carter uses it successfully with Year 3. Areas outside Britain are best studied later rather than sooner, in view of new geographical areas to be understood and the map work needed to understand this.

This will be the first time that children are involved in the BC/AD timing device unless 'Ancient Egypt' has been studied sooner, and it is often confusing to children as in BC, larger numbers are earlier in time than smaller ones which affects the use and construction of time-lines. If studied in Year 5 or 6, suitable units to complement it are 'Ancient Egypt', 'Romans, Anglo-Saxons and Vikings in Britain' and 'Ships and seafarers'. 'Ancient Egypt' and 'Ancient Greece', both in the BC part of the National Curriculum, could well be compared. 'Romans, Anglo-Saxons and Vikings in Britain', though just in the AD study, is concerned with the Romans who conquered Greece in the second century BC and then went on to add Britain to their Empire at the beginning of the first century AD. 'Ships and seafarers' is a good link since the Greeks had to be good sailors in view of the geographical shape of their peninsula and the many islands (e.g. Crete) belonging to them in the Aegean Sea.

If studied in Years 3 and 4, it is advisable to omit Greek religion, thought and literature and concentrate on myths/legends and everyday life in fifth century Athens. In other words, this unit is difficult for primary children and teachers alike. In retrospect, perhaps it should have been made an optional unit!

Unless this unit is to be viewed as a series of one-off topics, such as Greek gods, the Olympic Games or the Parthenon, teachers must know the outline of political events which gives a sense of wholeness and context to the depth topics. A rough time-line of decades and sequences may help (see Figure 14). More exact dates can be included for older juniors but this is not really necessary. Athens was at the height of her power as a city-state in the fifth century, known as the 'Classical period'. Two very helpful books on this chronology are *History: Timesavers* (Hughes and Cox, 1992 – see p. 113 for 'A time ribbon of key events') and *Practical Guides: History* (Hill and Morris, 1991 – for detailed dates pp. 99–100). Older juniors could also construct their own time-lines and a large one for the classroom. An understanding of geographical features and maps are also essential before detailed topics are studied. The mountainous nature of the peninsula is well illustrated in Collins' picture pack supporting the pupil's book on *Ancient Greece* (Worsnop, 1992). This shows the isolation of city-states in the valleys and the need for good ships to keep trade contact on the seaways. Many useful maps for 'Ancient Greece' can be

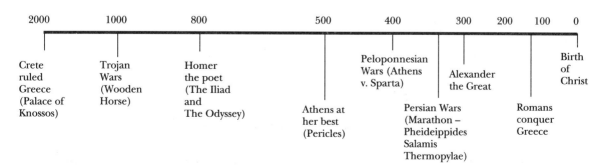

(**NB**   Spaces between dates do not accurately denote duration of time)

Figure 14   Time-line for 'Ancient Greece'

found in *Historical maps* (Hughes and Tweedie, 1993).

Some teachers may have told Greek myths and legends as stories to children in Key Stage 1, but few of these are intelligible to six-year-olds. The story of 'The Wooden Horse' and how the Greeks got into Troy may be an exception. This should be checked with Key Stage 1 teachers. Many of these stories involve most unlikely happenings and very long complicated names which makes retelling for sequencing difficult for children. Also the whole question of 'fact' and 'fiction' arises for the more enquiring minds. Which myths are classified as fantasy and imagination and which as legends in which there is an element of truth? A useful book is *Myths, Legends and Lore* (Lavender, 1975). It would seem better to reserve this storytelling/reading until the unit on 'Ancient Greece' is studied. The time-line in Figure 14 shows the myths and legends to have 'happened', if they did, long before the fifth century and some to be written down as poems by Homer in about 800 BC in the famous poems *The Iliad* (Siege of Troy) and *The Odyssey* (Travels of Odysseus or Ulysses on his way home from Troy). They would be re-told during the fifth century. The places connected with the stories have been excavated by archaeologists and found to be correct geographically. *History: Timesavers* (Hughes and Cox, 1992) provides a simple map of 'The Greek world of myths and legends' for children (p. 111). *Greek Heroes and Monsters* (Mason, 1991) can be read or listened to on an audio cassette. Teachers will find *The Faber Book of Greek Legends* (Lines, 1973; paperback, 1986) and charts in *Stories of the Past* (Pictorial Charts Educational Trust, 1993) a good background for the work.

Teachers should concentrate on fifth-century Athens to teach 'ways of life, beliefs and achievements', interspersing the topics with stories of myths and legends. The city-state of Athens under Pericles after the defeat of Persia introduced the first signs of 'democracy' which is very different from modern democracy. Only citizens were allowed to vote and they were small

in number. This does not preclude Greek citizens from having highly educated slaves who taught their children and acted as secretaries. Aesop was a Greek slave and his stories and fables may be read or told. During this period Pericles started to build the Parthenon on the hill of the Acropolis above Athens. The Piraeus, the port of Athens, was the centre of trade for merchant ships and warships. Detailed plans of Athens, the port and the land around could be used with older juniors. The Olympic Games, held in a purpose-built 'village', were started at Olympia. Plays were acted in the well-known semi-circular theatre at Epidaurus and gods and goddesses ruled the lives of Athenians, with sacrifices being offered to them and statues of them being erected. Greeks were heathen, not Christian. Herodotus who wrote of the Battle of Marathon is reckoned the first historian of all time. Homer was a poet. Plato and Socrates were the thinkers and philosophers who introduced discussion and argument into teaching. Euclid and Pythagoras discovered new ideas in mathematics. Plenty of recent resources show plans of houses and evidence gained from vases and sculptures. They also emphasise the lowly position of women in such war-like communities.

The 'legacy' of Greece to us today is not as obvious in practical terms as the legacy of the Romans or Victorians to Britain. Greek style 'classical' buildings such as the British Museum, the Elgin Marbles (most of the frieze of the Parthenon brought to Britain by Lord Elgin in 1803) in the British Museum and other precious artefacts in other museums are the concrete legacies. The Olympic Games held every four years in different parts of the world are an obvious second legacy. Greek plays in Greek-style theatre (usually outdoors), the writings of Herodotus, Homer and Plato in translation (and original) and the Greek language are less obvious legacies. Years 5 and 6 could undertake play acting, writings and language. Years 3 and 4 are better advised to study buildings, artefacts and sport. Comparison between Greek 'democracy' and modern Western democracy leads into the function of modern politics and may be possible, if controversial, with older juniors.

Russell Carter of Yaxley CE Junior School, Peterborough, writes of his work on Ancient Greece.

Ancient Greece: A cross-curricular history-based topic for Year 3

Prior to the advent of the National Curriculum we had not included topics about the ancient world in our curriculum, so it was after much discussion that we decided to include both 'Ancient Greece' and 'Ancient Egypt' in the Year 3 scheme of work. In some ways we felt that it would be better for older children but, on the other hand, we wanted to keep the chronological order of history topics we had been using for several years. Thus in 1991–2, we planned and worked through a term's topic based on 'The Ancient World', in which the relevant aspects of both civilisations were looked at concurrently and compared and contrasted with each other, and today, as the term progressed. The children enjoyed many aspects of this approach, but in 1992–3 we decided to spend consecutive half-terms on each unit. In this way we believed we would keep the civilisations separate but still able to compare and contrast them.

The 'Ancient Greece' unit came in the second half of the term, following that of 'Ancient Egypt'. This was because it was slightly longer and also we wished to make a visit to the Fitzwilliam Museum, in Cambridge, the focal point of the topic, and the Greek galleries were not available to us earlier.

Our initial planning was based on the grid suggested in the History Non-Statutory Guidance (1991) and was based on Key Issues or Questions which attempted to cover the way of life, beliefs and achievements of the period and thus include the various perspectives required as well as the important concepts. More detailed

planning was again shown on a grid using the headings already described in the case study of the 'Vikings'.

The first key issue was concerned with setting the scene and finding out about Greece today. Library books, holiday guides and the memories of parents and children from other years who had spent holidays in Greece helped to show how Greece is different from Britain. Atlases and wall maps were used to show the location of the country, in relation to both Britain and Egypt, thus there were strong links with geography skills and knowledge. Less time was spent on this aspect of the topic than had been spent on a similar introduction to Egypt, entirely due to the length of time available, but through group research and presentations, much was found out and many skills developed in a comparatively short time. A simple time-line of the period was completed and added to that showing the 'Ancient Egypt' period.

The visit to the Fitzwilliam Museum, of necessity, came very early in the topic but provided an excellent focal point for most of the key issues of the topic. By planning carefully and focusing the attention of the children quite sharply, it was possible to introduce questions such as:

- What would it have been like to live in Ancient Greece?
- How were the people ruled?
- What did people eat and wear?
- What sort of jobs did they do?
- What would it have been like for children?
- How did they entertain themselves?
- What did they believe in?
- How did religion affect their lives?
- What were the buildings like in Athens?

The sixty children worked in groups, each group researching one of the questions, and making careful notes and sketches to substantiate their findings. They were constantly reminded of the very important question, 'How do we know?' Some, but by no means all, of the focusing was assisted through worksheets, provided by the Education Service at the Fitzwilliam or by the school, which helped children to look meaningfully at the exhibits:

- Look at the pottery and see how many athletic events you can find.
- What sort of clothes did athletes wear?
- Do you think the painter saw this event or did he imagine it?
- Look at the painting of a Greek soldier. What armour is he wearing apart from his helmet?
- What do you think the armour was made of ?
- Draw the pieces of armour carefully.
- Look for different sorts of helmets and draw them.
- Look at the paintings on the pots and write down the jobs that people are doing.

Despite their young age, they were generally able to tackle this very well, benefitting from a previous similar experience in the 'Ancient Egypt' topic. The questions continued to be asked and researched on the return to school, and a substantial collection of resources, books, replica artefacts, posters and postcards had been built up for this purpose. The children worked individually or in small groups within their larger group and as the research progressed further links were made with other curriculum areas. Models of Greek buildings were designed and built, the children particularly enjoying making pillars reminiscent of those at the Fitzwilliam Museum. Clay pots were made and decorated, some with the help of drawings made at the museum or postcards from the British Museum as the source material, others showing scenes from life today which the children thought would give our ancestors a similar insight. Messages were written in Greek letters. Traditional Greek foods, such as taramasalata, tzatziki, halloumi and feta dip, were prepared and tasted, somewhat reluctantly on occasions. Role plays were devised showing the roles of rulers and the ruled, slaves and the free. Simple clothes and face masks were researched, designed and made to help in these. 'Eureka' became an 'in' word as young scientists followed in the footsteps of Archimedes. 'Olympic

games' were held and contested just as keenly as the ancient originals. Individuals and small working groups reported back and showed their work to each other and to the whole group, answered questions and explained 'how they knew'. In this way the Attainment Target was covered and the children assessed accordingly, care having been taken to provide for differentiation in the allocation of tasks. Extension activities were always prepared and available, within the context of the Key Issue, for the more able.

Other aspects of the topic were presented to the children on a whole-class basis, mainly through stories. These included such myths and legends as 'Theseus and the Minotaur', 'Jason and the Argonauts', 'Cyclops and Pegasus' as well as many of the events of the Persian Wars, with the Battles of Thermopylae and Salamis being particularly popular. Some of these were used as discussion points for looking at different viewpoints, leading on to informal drama activities.

The topic ended with a 'Greek day', in which the children shared their knowledge and experiences with the rest of the school and proved, beyond all doubt, the success of the topic. Perhaps older children would have been able to take some of the issues further, but that would be true of any topic or historical period. The children gained an interest, even love of history, which can now be built upon as they progress through Key Stage 2 and beyond.

The case-studies on 'The Vikings' and 'Ancient Greece' were undertaken by an experienced and dedicated primary historian. They may seem to set an unrealistically high standard for teachers less interested in these particular topics, but these two units are at present compulsory in the National Curriculum. Therefore, they do present a target for teachers to work towards over the years. The teacher concerned has been selective about content, as indeed I have been in writing about the other three units.

Key Stage 2 – Extension studies

Between World War I and World War II, M.V.C. Jeffreys wrote a seminal book *History in Schools: the Study of Development* (Pitman, 1939) which was to influence both primary and secondary teaching from that time onwards. His message was that children should not concentrate all their study on 'period' or 'patch' history, but should be able to see one element of the past in a 'line of development' and so 'interpret his own world as part of a larger whole'. It was assumed that such 'lines' existed. This led to courses being devised in which children studied for example clothes, transport or houses 'through the ages'. It was thought that through this chronological treatment children would acquire a concept of time. The 1994 Proposals provide for this in Extension study A. Teachers need knowledge of massive historical content if such work is to be successful; therefore the Non-Statutory Guidance (1991) is still much needed. Its suggestions are only claimed as 'starting-points for planning . . . they should not be seen as the only way of developing units and other approaches might be possible'.

Category A studies over a long period of time (no longer a thousand years as in 1991) have always been taught. Category B studies of a local theme have been developed very well since the 1960s. I question whether Category C studies (non-European) will, when added to the third-world localities rightly required in Key Stage 2

geography, require too much knowledge content from primary teachers. 'Ancient Egypt', a well-tried favourite, is an exception.

A new category of unit has been introduced in the 1994 Proposals: Category D, a study in depth. This is a most welcome development and gives greater flexibility in choice of content. Before 1991 the 'patch approach' was the most satisfactory treatment of history in the primary school. 'Topic work' was often based on a historical theme and other areas of the curriculum were integrated with it. Marjorie Reeves has immortalised this approach in her 'Then and There' series of small books written by specialists (Longman). Although originally published in the 1950s, some of these are still obtainable in a new edition. Her method book *Why History?* should be read and re-read as an inspiration to all teachers of history. She writes: 'Don't spread the butter too thinly all over; give it to them in lumps' (p. 53).

A study in depth gives children 'the historical experience' which is more important than 'learning history' (p. 24). Therefore, although Jeffreys and Marjorie Reeves advocate different ways of organising the learning of history, the 1994 Proposals cater for both. Lastly, remember that although all the Extension studies give more choice to teachers, they must 'extend and complement the core' (1994 Dearing Proposals, p. 8).

A STUDY – A LONG PERIOD OF TIME

This is the study of one theme over a long span of time. It should 'cover an important historical issue and compare developments in different periods and places'. No research has been done on what length of period is most suitable for children at different ages. At present we have to be content with knowing how children develop an understanding of a sequence of events rather than of a duration of time. Teachers should choose one of these A studies, use time-lines to cover the chosen period, and delve down to study familiar 'patches' mainly linked to the core units, with wider links if these are necessary, genuine, and with information readily available.

To date, there are few guidelines or published materials which are of much help. One way of planning suggested by Hill and Morris (Scholastic Press, 1991) is to get a child to keep a file for the A study and build up work on that topic each year to be pulled together in Year 5, hopefully by the coordinator or specialist. The other way of planning, favoured by *History in the National Curriculum* (Teaching History Research group, 1991) is to study the whole unit in Year 5 or 6 after most of the core units have been covered, as 'It is important not to dismantle the study units.' This could be linked to a local study such as a local historical house. When the extension study is selected, it should be favoured by the majority of a school's staff. Otherwise, if changes in staffing take place, resources collected for one study could become redundant.

My order of preference for a successful and easily prepared A study is either 'Ships and seafarers', 'Domestic life, families and childhood' or 'Houses and places of worship', still allowed in whole or part as an extension study A choice. Linda Holdridge and Cindy Bennett give a case-study of their work with Years 4, 5 and 6 in a mixed-age class over half a term, using 'Houses and places of worship' on page 56. 'Land transport' and 'Food and farming' are well catered for in good publications and can be treated in a similar way to 'Ships and seafarers'. Six themes may be selected for in-depth study, each theme being related to a core unit. In some cases it may be advisable to omit medieval history and the eighteenth century, as in the 1994 Proposals. An interesting addition would be 'School Days in Tudor and Stuart Times', offering two centuries as the 'long period of time' (see Figure 7, p. 37). With regards to the new 'Emigration and immigration' topic, I suggest that teachers who are interested await resource materials suitable for juniors. It could well link with core unit 4: 'Britain since 1930'.

Figure 15 shows a time-line for 'Ships and seafarers' from Viking ships to Victorian steamships and merchantmen. Six in-depth studies are shown, all concerned with important political issues. If 'a long period of time' is strictly adhered to, five themes could be selected. In this case and in 'Domestic life, families and childhood', the medieval period has been included on account of some excellent topics suitable for juniors. Emphasis should be placed on ship-building, and links with technology developed. Navigational instruments and maps are also indispensable as are the lives of sailors on the ships. I would omit trade, navies and colonies.

'Domestic life, families and childhood' from the Romans to the present day is an excellent 'line of development' and is covered in all the core units. It also links with 'Houses and places of worship' and Extension study B on a local theme. It can therefore reduce the preparation over the eight units. Figure 16 shows a suggested time-line with six themes. I suggest omitting 'families and rituals' and 'household interiors', both of which require specialised resources. This unit is one of the Extension studies suitable for study in Year 3 as a good link with the family life covered in Key Stage 1.

The case study below on 'Houses and places of worship' was carried out by Cindy Bennett (class teacher) and Linda Holdridge (History

Ships and seafarers AD

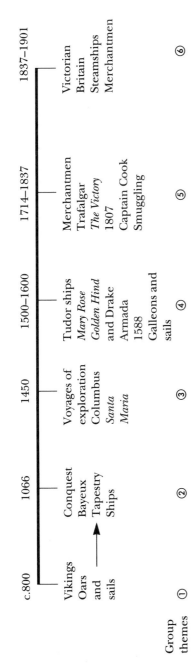

c.800	1066	1450	1500–1600	1714–1837	1837–1901
Vikings Oars and sails	Conquest Bayeux Tapestry → Ships	Voyages of exploration Columbus *Santa Maria*	Tudor ships *Mary Rose* *Golden Hind* and Drake Armada 1588 Galleons and sails	Merchantmen Trafalgar *The Victory* 1807 Captain Cook Smuggling	Victorian Britain Steamships Merchantmen
Group themes ①	②	③	④	⑤	⑥

Figure 15 Time-line for 'Ships and seafarers'

Domestic life, families and childhood AD

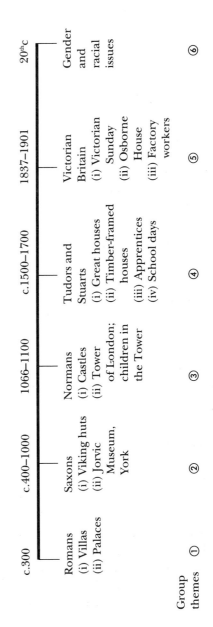

c.300	c.400–1000	1066–1100	c.1500–1700	1837–1901	20thc
Romans (i) Villas (ii) Palaces	Saxons (i) Viking huts (ii) Jorvic Museum, York	Normans (i) Castles (ii) Tower of London; children in the Tower	Tudors and Stuarts (i) Great houses (ii) Timber-framed houses (iii) Apprentices (iv) School days	Victorian Britain (i) Victorian Sunday (ii) Osborne House (iii) Factory workers	Gender and racial issues
Group themes ①	②	③	④	⑤	⑥

Figure 16 Time-line for 'Domestic life, families and childhood'

coordinator) of Highfield Primary School, Urmston, near Manchester for half a term. The 'long period of time' was covered through a time-line and individual buildings of varying periods were made by children. The main emphasis of work was houses from 1900 to the present day and the 'place of worship' was a visit to the local church. Therefore a selection was made from the suggestions in the Non-Statutory Guidance (1991). Linda Holdridge was pleasantly surprised how much this mixed-age group of less able children enjoyed the varied work of the 'line of development' and what good work came out of it.

Houses and places of worship

This study was undertaken by twenty-five Year 4, 5 and 6 children who all had some degree of learning difficulty. The average ability of the children was below that of the average eight- or nine-year-old. The topic was created in a cross-curricular way, as can be seen by the topic plan in Figure 17. We followed the general guidance given in Section F3 of the Non-Statutory Guidance of the Final Order of the History National Curriculum. The historical skills work as laid down by the Attainment Target was also kept in mind.

As the starting point of the topic, we looked at a time-line on homes from the caves of Early Man to the 1990s. Help with the illustrations was given by the worksheet in *Starting History – Homes* by Pat Hughes and Kath Cox (1991). The different homes were discussed in detail and the illustrations closely studied. This led to the children's realisation that homes progressed and developed through the ages which led to changes in lifestyle. The teacher reached this stage by careful questioning of the children's knowledge. A class time-line was made, starting with the two extremes – caves at one end and the new buildings, currently under construction on a site adjacent to the school, at the other. The teacher presented the children with a selection of illustrations of homes from the following ages:

Prehistoric, Iron Age, Roman, Medieval, Tudor, Georgian, Victorian, 1950s and the present day; and the children were asked to sequence these homes. This they were able to do well and much lively discussion ensued. The Georgian/Victorian homes were the ones which gave the most difficulty as to which came first. The sophistication of the Roman house compared with the Medieval one did not pass without comment. All the time the children's attention was being drawn to the architectural development of the housing style. Later the children chose one house from the time-line for individual study, and the knowledge gained was shared with the class, in writing, by drawings and verbally.

We then moved in on the period 1900 to the present day for a more detailed study of a home in the past, looking at, comparing and contrasting various aspects common to any period of home-life, for example, wash day, family life and entertainment, cooking, cleaning, etc. Here we must acknowledge the help and interest given by the book *At home in 1900* by Sallie Purkis (Longman, 1981). It was avidly read and taken home by most of the children. They especially enjoyed the real-life quotations in the book, which again led to much discussion about what it was like to have lived in 1900. During this topic there was a classroom display of nineteenth-century household implements such as a posser, a washtub, a washboard, carpet beater and a flat iron. Imaginative play was encouraged using these artefacts.

We have a building site adjacent to the school; this proved to be extremely useful and relevant for sequencing work. The idea of sequencing was introduced to the children by getting them to think of and draw themselves, as a baby, now, and in the future up to age seventy! (see Figure 19 on page 60.) With the sequencing idea firmly fixed, we moved on to the sequencing of building a house from foundations to roof. During the course of one week we watched the workmen complete the upper storey brickwork and window frames, followed by the fixing of the rafters and finally the tiling of the roof. The children went out daily to record the men at work. They took photographs and drew the sequence of the work in progress.

From this work we moved on to a study of doors and windows through the ages, learning the correct architectural terms. Armed with this knowledge the children became door and window detectives around the school and the immediate environment, looking for differences in door and window styles. One homework activity consisted of studying their own front door. The focus now switched to their own home. Graphs of the types of homes they lived in were done. They discussed their own homes, concentrating on the function of each room, comparing them with rooms from houses in the past, and finally ending up with a description/illustration of their own

---

Science
Materials bricks, sand, wood, cement, glass, metal, plastic, (suitability, strength).
Structure safe, strong doors/ windows: open/close, locks.
Use of services: gas, water, electricity.

Art
Junk modelling sewing, clay, painting, drawing.

History
Time line of homes from caves to now.
Looking at changes in buildings inside and out, compare photographs, illustrations e.g. 1900, 1950, present.
Changes?
Improvements?

Geography
Homes around the world: use of photos, pictures.

HOMES
CAVES ——— 1990s

English
Descriptive writing about own home, ideal home, home of the future, a haunted house.
Vocabulary for house parts and different types of houses, types of doors and windows.
Creative Writing class Poem – 'Home for me', story to finish from opening sentence – 'I looked up at the building in front of me ...'
Handwriting careful copying of Class Poem.
Stories for Listening Skills
Three Little Pigs, (by request!!)
House for All Seasons,
Norman's Ark.

Maths
Graphs types of houses we live in.
Shape buildings, doors, windows; tessellation of bricks, tiles.
Number house numbers, odd/evens, fractions ($\frac{1}{2}$, $\frac{1}{4}$); semi (detached).
Measurement for carpets, curtains, fitted units in kitchens,

Figure 17 Topic plan for 'Homes' within the unit 'Houses and places of worship'

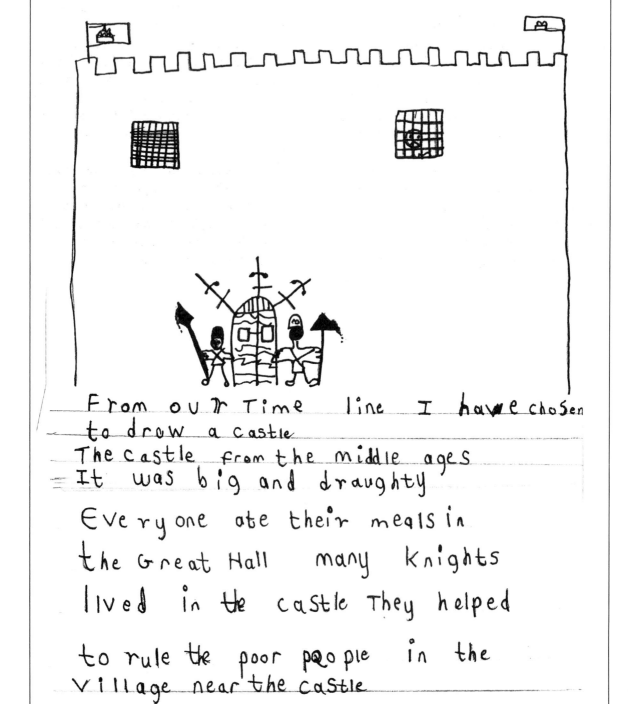

From our Time line I have chosen
to draw a castle.
The castle from the middle ages
It was big and draughty

Everyone ate their meals in
the Great Hall many knights
lived in the castle They helped

to rule the poor people in the
village near the castle

Figure 18 Michael's drawing of a castle

bedroom. Then, on into the future with an illustration/design of 'My ideal home in the future'.

We visited the local nineteenth-century parish church of St Clements in Urmston, with a ready-prepared worksheet to discover the architectural features and layout of a church. The vicar, the Rev. Alan Tiltman, showed the children around, explaining the function of the church furniture, for example, the font, the altar, pulpit, lectern, etc. He also explained the various celebrations and festivals throughout the church year. He allowed the children to handle and make inferences from the various artefacts used in the communion service. Rev. Tiltman also talked to the children about the history of the church, showing the changes in the building in the last one hundred and twenty-five years.

Visits to a synagogue and mosque were planned in order to make links with world history, but these had to be abandoned as the teacher broke her foot during the time of this study and operations were directed from home, or from crutches! We also planned to visit the Old Hall at Tatton Hall, near Knutsford, where there is a suite of rooms set out to illustrate the changes in houses and rooms from medieval times to the present day, but this had to be abandoned for the same reason.

All the work described above was reinforced by artwork, including photographs taken by the children of the builders, general painting and drawings of the topic, 3D models of houses and churches, stained glass window patterns and sewn appliqué work of buildings.

Figure 19   Sequencing: 'What will you be like at 70?' – Jamie's life

B STUDY – LOCAL HISTORY

In one sense, all history is local history as events have to happen in one place. In academic circles it has come to mean one particular brand of the past and an illustration of national and world history. How local the past is, depends upon the event, person and period being studied. For example, the Roman settlement in Manchester cannot be understood without a study of the Romans in the North West as far as Hadrian's Wall. On the other hand, the history of a street or a village can more easily be thought of as an entity. For the last twenty years, local history has been studied very well in many primary schools. Examples of excellent work done in history and geography are detailed in the chapter 'Good Practice Observed' in *The Teaching of History and Geography* (DES, 1989) and in unusually attractive books using personal experience – *Village Heritage* (Pinnell, 1986) and 'History Around You', Allan Waplington's well-known series for children (1986), linked to Granada television. Children's close observation and detailed use of a variety of primary sources has begun to make them into skilled historians. The tendency to over-concentrate on local history and to view 'history' as synonymous with 'local history' throughout the five-to-eleven year span, has been balanced by the National Curriculum.

Schools are to attempt one study of local history. This type of study involves the teacher in much hard work and reference to libraries, record offices and museums, as there are usually few nationally published materials which fit one's own locality. Sources should be carefully checked for accessibility and ease of use by junior children, probably in Years 5 and 6. Handwriting before 1700 is difficult to read, and some old maps are not clear enough to use for finding your way during fieldwork (see Figure 6, p. 36). Local history is perhaps the best way to prepare for using historical sources in extension study 'D', a study in depth.

According to the 1994 Dearing Proposals, the local study should cover a long period of time (several centuries); a short period of time (several decades); or 'an aspect of the local community which illustrates developments taught in other study units.' A long period might cover buildings in one village or town over several centuries (see Chapter 9). A short period could include the siege of a castle or town, the Civil War of the seventeenth century in one locality, or the development of a factory or a seaside resort in the nineteenth century. It could also include the local consequences of emigration and immigration since 1945. As part of whole-school planning, teachers should select all the extension studies at the same time as the four core units and decisions should be made as to how and where in the four Key Stage 2 years they should be studied. It is to be hoped that seven-year-olds will already have enjoyed some local study involving family and oral history in the infant school. If a turnpike road is selected (for example the Liverpool-Prescot-Warrington Road), 'Land transport' should be chosen as the extension study A, since this topic, mainly related to the eighteenth century, will not link with any Key Stage 2 core unit. In the same way a Cistercian monastery founded in the thirteenth century could be linked to extension study A: 'Churches and places of worship'.

Any local study involves using geographical skills related to places and themes. These are now combined in the new single Attainment Target for geography. Study of the school locality itself is to be required in geography at both Key Stages (SCAA 1994b, pp. 3, 5). Fieldwork, away from the school area in a contrasting locality, is an excellent basis for a combination of history and geography.

In planning all studies, care should be taken to use the local study for cross-curricular purposes introducing technology, English, science and art wherever possible. At what age the local study should be carried out depends upon the whole jigsaw of the other units, particularly the long

Extension study A, if a long local unit is chosen. An in-depth study of a short period is usually easier for younger children to handle. According to a leading local historian, the nineteenth century is 'the richest period for the study of English local history' (Rogers, 1972). Therefore a study of a factory apprentice in a particular local factory is a suitable link with 'Victorian Britain' (core unit 3). A long local study unit together with an Extension study A are, together, a good way of pulling together all the British core units in Year 5.

Choice of a short or long local history unit much depends upon the locality of the school and interest of the teacher. Personal interest and enthusiasms are particularly important. Here are some suggestions for the long period of several hundred years around the topic of either a building or a person. Buildings might be the magnificent Fishbourne Roman Palace near Chichester, St Albans Abbey (with its excellent education centre) or Quarry Bank Mill in Styal, Cheshire. Fishbourne and Quarry Bank link into British core units through Roman ways of life and child apprentices in nineteenth-century factories. St Albans Abbey should be studied alongside Extension study A 'Houses and places of worship'. A person could be studied as the centre of a long unit, and could include Bess (Elizabeth Shrewsbury) and her famous Hardwick Hall, associated with Mary Queen of Scots and Elizabeth I, or an alternative could be the Cecil family and Hatfield House, ranging from the sixteenth century to the political figures of the nineteenth century.

Short periods of several decades are easier to handle because they are more specific. As in a long study, a person or a building could be central to the study, but in addition could be an important stirring event. The building might be a particular cinema in your town from its birth in the 1930s to its conversion into a bingo hall in the 1970s – an important landmark of social life in that period. On the other hand, one could use a Nonconformist chapel (c.1840–1914) or a half-timbered Tudor house, such as Speke Hall near Liverpool, from the end of Elizabeth I's reign (1580) to the Restoration of 1660. Manchester schools could choose Mrs Emmeline Pankhurst (using the new Pankhurst Museum) or Cambridgeshire schools, Oliver Cromwell using the Cromwell Museum at Huntingdon. Mrs Pankhurst, in the Edwardian period, should be linked with extension study A 'Domestic life, families and childhood', since 1901–30 is not part of the core National Curriculum. Stirring events can form excellent short periods. They may only be of one day duration, such as the Peterloo Massacre in St Peter's Fields, Manchester, in 1819, linking with the whole question of parliamentary reform in nineteenth-century Britain. An alternative could be the Siege of Chester (1643–6) when William Brereton defeated Charles I's army at Rowton Moor. A third possible event might be the building of the Manchester-Liverpool Railway in 1829–30, linking it to 'Land transport', an extension study A. Those living in the north-east of Britain might prefer to use the building of the Stockton-Darlington Railway in 1825.

Thus, Extension study B is the most open-ended of all the units in the National Curriculum. It has natural links with most other units, as a local study is a microcosm of national and world history. More detailed help on the sources for children to use may be found in my book *History in Primary Schools* (Open University Press, 1990).

C STUDY – NON-EUROPEAN SOCIETY

The non-European units in the 1994 Dearing Proposals are 'Ancient Egypt', 'Mesopotamia' (now mercifully combined with Assyria), 'The Indus Valley', 'The Maya', 'Benin', and 'The Aztecs'. The last five may be easier to undertake when more material is published. One such publication is the well-presented *An Introduction to the Non-European Study Units* (NCC, 1993). Let us hope that, in a new edition, the seven pages on Assyria will be replaced by equally clear pages on the Aztecs. For the purposes of this book, I am concentrating on 'Ancient Egypt' and 'The Aztecs'.

Ancient Egypt

Ancient Egypt has been a well-tried and successful topic in primary schools for many years. There are excellent and available resources, particularly linked to archaeological evidence, which schools already own. Although there are few buildings to visit in Britain, the British Museum and many other museums possess excellent artefacts and cater well for school visits through their publications (see Russell Carter's account of his visit to the Fitzwilliam Museum, Cambridge on pp. 65–6). The time-span, as in Ancient Greece, is very great and a time-line should begin any study of Ancient Egypt (see Figure 20 overleaf). The period usually studied is that of the rule of the Pharaohs (3000–1000 BC) before Egypt was overrun by Persia and Alexander the Great of Greece. After then, the House of Ptolemy ruled ending with Queen Cleopatra, whose entanglement with Roman generals led to conquest by Rome, and Egypt becoming part of the Roman Empire. There are good obvious links with the Old Testament, geography and technology, slightly less obvious ones with botany. There are good reasons for studying 'Ancient Egypt' with 'Ancient Greece', 'Food and farming', and possibly 'Writing and printing'. The only problem is that 'Ancient Greece' is better studied

in Year 5 or 6, whereas 'Ancient Egypt' is within the grasp of Year 3 or 4. All topics listed in the 1991 Final Order are suitable for younger children, but certain resource books are more attuned to older juniors. The focus of the unit is the same as unit 5, 'the ways of life, beliefs and achievements', which makes comparison sensible between Egypt and Greece, especially as they are both concerned with BC and were both conquered by the Romans. Some teachers may want to concentrate on Tutankhamun's tomb in Years 3 or 4 and study other parts of Egypt with Greece later.

A natural link with geography is the position of Egypt in the world. Remember that it is part of Africa. The dominance of the River Nile over all Egyptian life is an easy concept; the course of the river and its delta is easy to draw and copy for younger children. With no made-up roads, the Nile was the only means of transport, and ships were essential to the Egyptians. The Nile flooded for four months of each year and provided soil for growing crops on pasture land on either side of the river for the rest of the year. The Egyptians invented the *shadoof* for raising water from the Nile and for irrigation purposes for the very dry seasons. They were economical and expert farmers on the small amount of land which was not desert.

Egyptian society was hierarchical, as it was in Greece. Pharaohs were considered gods, the nobility lived luxurious lives, and scribes interpreted and wrote hieroglyphic writing and taught children and priests. Craftsmen created the huge statues and beautiful jewellery worn by the wealthy. Ordinary Egyptians did most of the hard work, helped by slaves who were the lowest rung of the social system (much more so than in Greece). Women had no power, as in Greece, with the exception of the wives of the pharaohs (such as Nefertiti) and the few pharaohs who were women (such as Hatshepsut). Egyptians lived in mud-baked houses of differing sizes and the wealthy enjoyed entertainments from

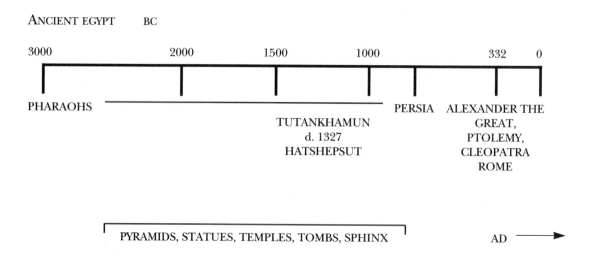

Figure 20   Time-line for 'Ancient Egypt'

musicians, dancers and games such as draughts and senet, as well as exotic foods.

One important reason for studying Ancient Egypt is the buildings, which were planned by skilful engineers and erected by slave labour over many years. No European country BC has left us such enduring epitaphs as the Step and Great Pyramids, the Sphinx at Giza and other huge statues. Archaeologists still find Egypt a treasure trove for their work which provides artefacts as good evidence to be understood by most juniors, so satisfying the needs of the Attainment Target. When robbers stole too much from the pyramids, the Egyptian builders then turned their expertise to tombs underground to house their precious belongings. These were also robbed but Howard Carter found one that was almost unspoilt when he discovered Tutankhamun's tomb in 1922. The unique buildings of the Egyptians make a good comparison with classical Greece and western European civilisation. They are more simple and easily modelled by young children.

Before 3000 BC, Egyptian writing or hieroglyphics had begun. This art was further understood by the writing carved onto the Rosetta Stone, now in the British Museum. This stone had Greek, Egyptian and demotic (popular Egyptian)

writing on it on the same topic. Greek scholars learnt about hieroglyphics from this. It is easy for children to make up this writing as one picture is a word. It was written on papyrus with reed pens. Most of the new resource books show how children can make papyrus and reed pens and so write their name and a few sentences in hieroglyphs.

One of the most popular in-depth studies is the whole question of Egyptian gods/goddesses and death. This led Egyptians to believe in a very practical after-life when all important people needed their favourite belongings round them. A 'book of the dead' was usually found in each tomb to help a dead person to find his way to heaven. Mummified bodies were put in pyramids and tombs. The greatest find was the tomb of Tutankhamun in the Valley of the Kings at Thebes, discovered by Howard Carter in 1922. The majority of the finds are in the Cairo Museum, but other museums have valuable examples of Egyptian artefacts (notably the Museum of Manchester University). So much archaeological information is available that this could be the central topic in a study of Egypt. It has links with botany through much research into the dried flowers found in the tomb.

Tutankhamun's body was garlanded in fresh flowers which were three thousand years old. Professor Frayling's television series (1993) also links Tutankhamun to the present century in ways ranging from Egyptian-style clothes to the Egyptian Hall at Harrods store. Below, Russell Carter of Yaxley CE Junior School in Peterborough gives an account of his work on Ancient Egypt.

Ancient Egypt: A cross-curricular history-based topic for Year 3

This topic was carried out by a group of sixty Year 3 children during the school year 1992–3. 'Ancient Egypt' had been an integral part of a topic on Ancient Civilisation in the previous year, but for reasons referred to in the 'Ancient Greece' case study, was carried out in the first part of the Spring Term 1993, followed immediately by 'Ancient Greece', thus allowing for comparisons to be made between the two, and present-day civilisations.

The initial planning for the topic followed the formula described in previous case studies and was based around the following key questions:

- What do we know about Egypt?
- How is it different from Britain?
- What does 'ancient' mean – how long ago was it?
- Why was the Nile important to the Egyptians?
- What was it like to be a pharaoh?
- How did other people live?
- What did people believe in?
- Why were their gods so important?
- How did they write?
- What was their art like?
- How were the pyramids built?
- What important things happened in Ancient Egypt?
- How is Egypt different today?
- How do we know?

By posing these questions, we felt that we were meeting the requirements of the National Curriculum by looking at different perspectives, everyday lives and introducing the children to archaeological evidence.

A short introduction to the topic saw Egypt being 'discovered' on large-scale maps and then its shape, size, physical features, climate and people being compared to Britain. Next came an attempt to set up a time-line showing how long ago we mean by 'ancient' Egypt. The children had previously been introduced to, and set up, time-lines of their own, their parents' and their grandparents' lifetimes, so they had a good understanding of the concept, but it was still difficult for them to understand the time-scale involved. Using the time of Jesus as a pointer was very helpful. Initially, a washing-line time-line, using pegs, proved useful as it went almost all the way around the school and at least indicated to them that it was a very long time ago!

A visit to the Egyptian galleries at the Fitzwilliam Museum, Cambridge, was to be the starting point for the key questions above and consequently this took place very early on in the topic. The visit gave a very good insight into the period for the children, who were fascinated with the exhibits, particularly those to do with Egyptian gods and the preparations for an after-life. Notes were taken and sketches made.

On returning to school, it was still this aspect which enthralled the children, and changes were quickly made to our original planned order of working through the key questions, and after periods of discussion with the children the following questions were posed and tasks provided.

How was a mummy prepared?

The children were encouraged to build on what they had found out at the museum through researching the many reference books, posters and postcards which had been provided for them. One published scheme by Jane Shuter and Pat Taylor – *Ancient Civilizations Pack*, Our World, Heinemann (1991) – provides a worksheet showing the preparation sequence, but not in the correct order, and this proved very useful for some children.

Design a mummy case
This was what the children were anxious to get on with following the museum visit, and again research took place before a wide variety of materials, including papier mâché, cardboard and boxes, washing-up liquid bottles, clay and bandages, were used to perform the tasks. Research then took place on the designs to be used to decorate the cases, and these were practised on paper before being transferred onto the cases using a PVA paint. Hieroglyphics were also used and this led to the children writing and translating messages to each other in this form. Some children then wanted to research, design and make their own canopic jars and heart scarabs, both of which had fascinated them at the museum. The completed mummies and cases formed an excellent display, made more interesting by the diversity of size, which created a great deal of discussion as the various drawings and designs were explained. Questions were asked as to whether everyone, including pharaohs would have the same sort of mummy case.

What did the Egyptians take with them into the after-life?
The children were asked to research, list and draw the items which the Egyptians had thought necessary to take with them into the after-life and to say why they were taken. Some children found out a lot about the food ancient Egyptians ate and prepared samples of it. Shabti figures were also researched, designed and drawn or made. An extension to this aspect was then carried out, with the children discussing and deciding what they would take with them into the after-life if they had the same beliefs.

Why were mummified animals, particularly cats, found in many tombs?
The more able children relished finding the answer to this and went on to research many of the Egyptian gods.

How do we know?
By a mixture of the reading and telling of the story of the finding of the tomb of Tutankhamun, the children learned a great deal about the work of archaeologists and the use of evidence. Some of this was followed up as role-play and a group of children began to 'excavate' a corner of the school field, finding much evidence of the past but nothing Egyptian!

This in turn led to a very short period on 'how the pyramids were built'. Pyramid shapes were constructed and many experiments set up to find out how the stones could have been moved without modern machinery. Mathematical work on shape, size and volume proved very useful.

Now we had run out of time, and at first thought that we had not covered our initial key questions, but on evaluating the topic, we were surprised just how much had been covered. We had certainly met the requirements of the Extension unit. The children had also been given opportunities to gain experience within all the history Attainment Target and we, the teachers, had learned a great deal about assessing children's work, particularly evidence and bases of attainment. Most important of all, however, the children had gained a real interest in finding out about the past. Hopefully we will be able to develop this further in topics on other historical periods.

The Aztecs

Those teachers who have had time to prepare adequately and are enthusiastic about the study, particularly as a cross-curricular topic (Horton, 1992), may wish to devote more time to it. One advantage is the link with geography and the essential study of old and modern maps of the world so ably shown in the Scholastic publication *Historical Maps* (Hughes and Tweedie, 1993). In any case, it is best attempted in Year 6 together with 'Life in Tudor Times' and 'Ships and seafarers'. However, the case-study from Bristol suggests that younger children could enjoy it. I would support treating the Aztec civilisation and Spanish conquest as part of a time-line leading to the Spanish Conquest, Spanish Empire and more trade between America and Europe. *History: Timesavers* by Pat Hughes and Kath Cox (1992) provides very adequate coverage for this type of treatment.

The whole question of bias, exploitation and multicultural concerns can loom large in this unit and can almost become out of proportion. Interpretations of the past have to be carefully handled. Views of contemporary Spaniards and Aztecs can be found in written source material in most of the published packs/books, but the present-day views of Columbus, his intentions and methods, and Cortes in his deceitful approach to Montezuma, the Aztec ruler, have been very aggressively portrayed in the media. The extremes of viewpoints should be treated with care by teachers who are well read in the period. Discussion can lead to children thinking that all people of the past were selfish, greedy and cruel. It is as well to remember that Thomas More, Erasmus and Martin Luther lived at the same time.

Emphasis has been laid on the material examples of Aztec craftsmanship and buildings, as it does in Ancient Greece and Egypt, but, as in India and Africa today, many of these marvels were made by slaves for their masters. Much as children are said to glory in bloodshed and love tales of battles, they cannot help but be dismayed at the cruel blood sacrifices of Aztecs to their gods resulting in 250 000 murders a year, and the injustice of their social hierarchy, as in the study of Greece and Egypt. Women had a particularly hard time in all three materially brilliant civilisations. Comparison of these conflicting attitudes in the three units could well be discussed in Year 6, but teachers need to know enough about each unit to initiate this cross-unit discussion. Conquest of the Aztecs by Cortes, both blood-thirsty and bizarre, has parallels in other parts of history. William of Normandy pretended

to run away at Hastings and so draw Harold's men down from their safe hill position. In the same period of history we find Drake pretending to attack the Spaniards in Calais harbour by sending in eight fireships (unit 2). If discussion takes place about 'right' and 'wrong', accepted methods of war at the time must be included. Knowing the mind of your enemy is essential in all warfare.

A project was funded in 1992 by the National Council for Educational Techonology (NCET) and the University of the West of England at Bristol to experiment with three primary schools undertaking work on The Aztecs. The children were in varying age groups from seven to eleven, one being of mixed age and ability. In each school the work took one term and much time was spent at computers by groups of children and individuals. The project was run by Penelope Harnett and colleagues from the University of the West of England with Cabot Primary School, Mangotsfield Primary School and Romney Avenue Junior School, all of Bristol. An account of their work follows.

Exploration and encounters 1450–1550

The value of IT for historical investigations is emphasised in the 1991 History Non-Statutory Guidance: 'IT can help pupils investigate historical sources otherwise unavailable to them or difficult and time consuming to analyse. IT can help with historical enquiry and in communicating the results of historical study' (NSG, p. C13). As the project developed it was found that IT did become an integral part of the children's learning; it was a great motivating factor and also gave children different opportunities for acquiring information and recording their findings.

The study was introduced and set within a time context in different ways by the schools. One school used the programme *Timelines* which enabled children to key in their own information to create their own time-line. Another school used the device of a time machine to place the study unit in context. Using the programme *Extra*, the teacher typed different clues into the computer. The clues referred to different dates stretching back from the present to 1520 and the children were expected to identify the date using books and other reference material. Clues began with children's own experiences; for example, the initial clue referred to their first day in school (1987): 'There are children arriving. Their clothes look very similar to those of today. Some of the children look very worried. It looks as if it is the first day of term. The headteacher is welcoming some of the children. The reception teacher is talking to some parents.'

Another clue referred to Queen Victoria's Golden Jubilee: 'The girls are all wearing dark dresses. Many have white over-aprons. They are sitting in rows. Oh dear, a boy is being caned for being late. Now the children are learning a song for the Golden Jubilee.' Work on the clues provided many opportunities for discussion, and the activity gave a real purpose for developing information retrieval skills. Children were involved in skimming and scanning texts and using indices to locate key words.

If the children became stuck, they moved onto the next clue and returned later to the difficult clue, recognising now that the date they needed would be between two dates which they had already identified. The activity gave good experience in moving about in time and the opportunity to see the inter-relationship between events. There is a variety of evidence available for work on this study.

Written accounts of the conquest from the Spanish point of view can be found in works by Diaz and Cortes. Aztec accounts were passed on by word of mouth and written down by Spanish friars living in Mexico later in the sixteenth century. Cortes' description of the market was used by one teacher as a basis for a huge collage. The children read the passage carefully and conducted some of their own research as to what the products for sale would look like, before embarking on the collage. They questioned the

number of people mentioned (60 000) and wondered if this was an exaggeration. The children concluded it probably was, since often people say more than they actually mean. One child had a friend who often said 'hundreds' when he possibly only meant 'ten'! The reliability of the sources was questioned on another occasion when a school was investigating the arrival of Spaniards. One child was intrigued to find three different numbers relating to the size of the Spanish forces; why were there so many discrepancies and which was the correct figure?

There are many pictures available of Aztec artefacts and buildings for children to work from. However, pictures do not always convey the actual size of an object. The massive structures of the temples need some reference point so that children can appreciate their height and recognise the impressive technological feats of the Aztecs. One school tried to plot the temple of Technochtitlan in the playground but found that they ran out of space!

Computer simulations of the voyage and the conquest of Mexico were used by the children, (Tressell's *Explorations and Encounters 1991*). The simulation of the voyage was used as a starting point for drama in one school. Using the source material within the pack, children organised their voyage, loaded stores and played out the various hazards which they encountered as they crossed the Atlantic. The activity provided a motive for carefully researching the details of the voyage, and also provided opportunities for children to collaborate and to develop shared understandings of the period.

The simulations also enabled children to investigate different points of view on the arrival of the Spaniards. Aztec and Spanish views were explored by taking on the roles of advisors to either 'Angry Lord' or Cortes. These advisors drew on several sources of information as they considered the advice which they wanted to give.

A newsroom simulation, using the programme *Teletype*, was also used for children to experience the different viewpoints of the Aztecs waiting for news of the invaders and of the Spaniards sending reports of their explorations back to Spain. The simulation began with an initial message to the Aztecs: 'Strange beings have come from the sea. Strange four-legged monsters have been seen with human bodies on their backs.' At the same time the Spaniards were being informed: 'Cortes has landed at Vera Cruz – he is marching his army to Tenochtitlan.' More reports followed at ten-minute intervals which gave the children time to research what was happening as the scenario unfolded. Books, pictures, posters, postcards and tapes were all used to resource the children's enquiries. Having two groups of children working on opposite sides produced interesting discussions and did help them to develop an awareness of how different interpretations might arise. In turn this led the children to question their sources of evidence, 'How do we know so much about what happened that long ago?'

It would appear that the order in which the topic is introduced to children can influence how children view different events. One school began with an investigation of the Aztec civilisation and the teacher noticed the children's identification with the Aztecs and their horror at the arrival of the Spaniards and the destruction of the wonderful Aztec treasures. These children really questioned whether the arrival of the Spaniards was a good thing and this contrasted with views expressed by children in another school where the topic had been introduced with the voyages of discovery. In this second school the children accepted the fate of the Aztecs and did not question the Spanish role in the destruction of a culture.

The study provided teachers with many opportunities for addressing the different level descriptions. Comparisons of now and then in terms of domestic life, fashion, ships and navigators were explored. More complex ideas of change and cause and effect were introduced as children discussed the pace of the destruction of Aztec culture and the ravages of disease. The

discovery of different foods and its long-term effect on trade and on people's eating patterns was investigated. Copies of old maps were photocopied onto overhead transparencies and placed on top of each other so that children could identify changes in people's perceptions of the world following the voyages of exploration. Children were encouraged to recognise the distinctive features of Aztec culture and one school found that children were able to cross-reference their findings across different periods of time, and that when they were making mosaics of Aztec artefacts, the children noted that they were using a similar technique to that which they had encountered when studying the Romans. There were significant differences, however; Roman mosaic pieces were stuck in clay and were larger than those of the Aztecs, who used gum to fix their pieces. The children were fascinated by this observation – why were there such similarities across different periods of time and in different areas of the world? This led to other interesting discussions, for example, the pyramids in Egypt were compared with some of the Aztec constructions.

Children recorded their findings in a variety of ways. Opportunities for artwork were abundant; a large frieze was made of an Aztec crowd; collages made of the Aztec gods; Aztec patterns were copied and children attempted to make some Aztec pots. Close observational drawings were made of different fruit and vegetables such as peppers, chillies, avocados and maize.

Some schools used the software programme *Touch Explorer Plus* (1989) and invited children to enter information about the sailing ships on an outline of a ship drawn on an overlay for a concept keyboard. The information included names for different parts of the ship and descriptions of the work undertaken in the different areas. In a mixed-age class, the older children entered information into the programme which younger children then used as a source of information for their own work. This gave a real purpose for entering information into the computer. Following the newsroom simulation on the Spanish arrival, the children wrote different reports for Spanish and Aztec newspapers, using the programme *Typesetter* (1987).

At the end of term, children from the three schools (Cabot Primary School, Mangotsfield Primary School and Romney Avenue Junior School, all in Bristol) visited Penelope Harnett and colleagues from the University of the West of England for an 'Aztec afternoon'. Graciela Sánchez and Ian Mursell from Mexicolore introduced the children to a range of 'hands-on' activities related to the culture of ancient and modern Mexico. The activities included dressing-up in traditional costumes, preparing food, making traditional Mexican music and learning a Mexican dance. Other activities were organised by tutors and students. Children were invited to design their own glyphs, using textured paper similar to the paper made from bark used by the Aztecs. A facsimile copy of the Codex Nutall was used as a basis for their designs. A large outline map which included Spain, West Africa and Central America was laid out on the floor, and

children compared the large outlines with maps in the atlas and were encouraged to predict the distance across the Atlantic. Having reached some decisions, the children used control technology and programmed a 'Roamer' to cross the ocean and return to Europe. Other children played board games devised by students using beans for counters and being rewarded with pieces of chocolate.

The afternoon concluded with a ceremony to the god of rain Tlaloc, and tutors, dressed as priests, asked Tlaloc to bless the maize crops with sufficient water. The ceremony was based on the June festival of Etzalqualizli during which the ancient Aztecs used to make a porridge from beans and maize (Etzalli) and distribute it to the crowds. The children were summoned to participate in the celebrations by the beat of the drum, and crops such as tomatoes, chillies, peppers and maize were brought to the god and prayers said over the offerings. The children drank pineapple juice and tasted festival food, including guacamole, made from avocados, and porridge made from beans and maize spread onto tortilla chips.

D STUDY – A STUDY IN DEPTH

The 1994 Dearing Proposals require the depth study to 'cover an important historical issue' and to be related to a unit already studied. I very much welcome the suggested study of Mary Queen of Scots (see p. 37) although not of James I. This is an opportunity to introduce some seventeenth-century work not now in core unit 2. The 'reformer' could be Oliver Cromwell (1649–58), a much-neglected character of great interest to older juniors if treated with imagination. He tried to reform politics, the church and morals; his rule was a 'watershed' in English history: the man who refused the offer of the crown of England. But there was another side

to him too (p. 16). An exciting approach is taken by John Cooper and Susan Morris in *The Cromwell Family*, in the 'World of Change' series (Stanley Thorne 1987). This shows the link between the Tudor Thomas Cromwell, of the dissolution of the monasteries, and Oliver Cromwell who defeated Charles I in the Civil War.

John Bunyan, another religious visionary, could well be the subject of a study in depth. His famous *Pilgrim's Progress* is an excellent contemporary source, reflecting Bedfordshire scenery. The simplicity of the story of a pilgrim seeking salvation can appeal to children. A Tudor and Stuart house provides a compact study in depth and could link with the local study B. Schools near Hampton Court Palace, Hatfield House, Carisbrooke Castle or a National Trust property might continue to use resource material already tried out successfully. Recently published resources include *A Stuart House*, in the 'Let's Discover' series by Ruth Thomson (Franklin Watts, 1993), and *Tudor Farm House* by Elizabeth Newbury, in the 'What Happened Here?' series. (A and C Black, 1994). Other obvious examples linked to the core units are the Sutton Hoo Ship Burial (A Care Evans *The Sutton Hoo Ship Burial* British Museum publications, 1994), Hadrian's Wall (English Heritage), and King Arthur and the Knights of the Round Table (John Matthews and Bob Stewart *Warriors of Arthur* (Blandford Press, 1987).

This type of study gives plenty of scope for using contemporary sources relating to local and national history such as Roman tombstones, legends of King Arthur, inventories (list of goods attached to wills), diaries, letters and census returns. Years 5 and 6 children should have developed their information retrieval skills as well as abilities to use source material. Therefore it is at this upper junior stage that the study in depth should be undertaken. The enthusiasm of the children will probably necessitate a 'spill-over' into the one day free from the National Curriculum. Extension study D is a teacher's dream come true!

Although the 1994 Dearing Proposals make clear that more time should be spent on the four core units, teachers may well be more interested in preparing their own themes allowed by the new extension studies. These are very flexible and clearly expressed. Study D gives tremendous scope for initiative. But if this flexibility is to be used with history in mind, it must not be construed as an invitation to return to the open-ended topic work of pre-1991. Rather, it should be seen as a stimulus to attend in-service courses and to learn how to be historians. Such teachers will be trusted to assess children's progress responsibly at the end of each Key Stage.

PART III

Other implications of the National Curriculum

The National Curriculum Order provides a useful checklist that can
be applied to the plan for the Key Stage:

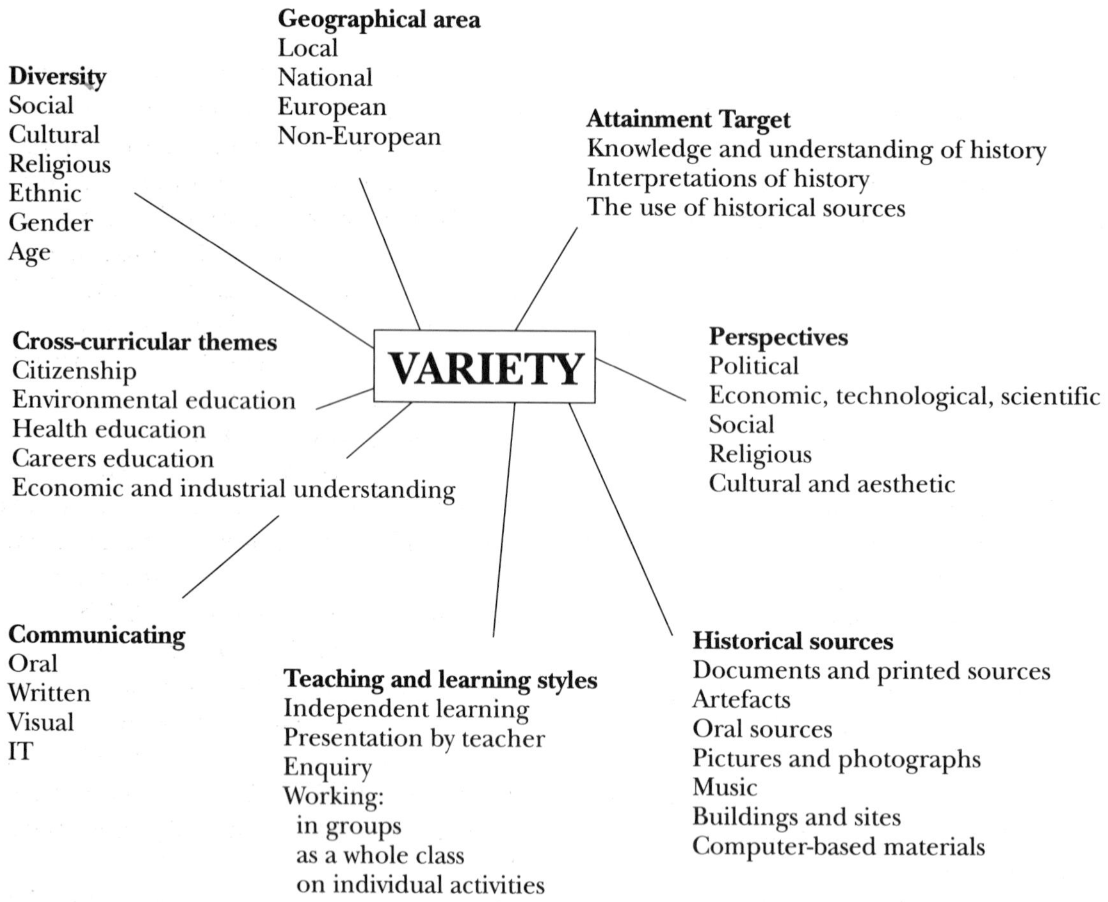

Geographical area
Local
National
European
Non-European

Diversity
Social
Cultural
Religious
Ethnic
Gender
Age

Attainment Target
Knowledge and understanding of history
Interpretations of history
The use of historical sources

Cross-curricular themes
Citizenship
Environmental education
Health education
Careers education
Economic and industrial understanding

VARIETY

Perspectives
Political
Economic, technological, scientific
Social
Religious
Cultural and aesthetic

Communicating
Oral
Written
Visual
IT

Teaching and learning styles
Independent learning
Presentation by teacher
Enquiry
Working:
 in groups
 as a whole class
 on individual activities

Historical sources
Documents and printed sources
Artefacts
Oral sources
Pictures and photographs
Music
Buildings and sites
Computer-based materials

Each topic/study unit will have its own 'unique blend' of some of
these aspects of variety, and should, together, achieve balance
across the Key Stage

Figure 21   Variety – history in the whole curriculum at Key Stage 2 (Devon Local Education Commitee)

History in the whole curriculum

Teachers may find history the most difficult subject to fit into the primary curriculum in spite of having only one Attainment Target. The detailed yet vague content specification of the eight units is threatening, and it is difficult to see how these units relate to the integrated curriculum which is the experience of most teachers. These fears may arise from lack of time to find out the historical content of the units or from an inability to realise that history is an umbrella subject which can be a unifying discipline for the whole curriculum.

The Discussion Paper produced by the 'Three Wise Men', Robin Alexander, Tim Rose and Chris Woodhead (1992), emphasises that 'spending more time on basic language and number skills will not necessarily help children to reach higher standards if the quality of teaching is not present'. Norman Thomas (1992) writes 'breadth of content should not be seen as being in opposition to teaching children to read, write and calculate'. He implies that certainly older juniors can improve their reading by 'informational factual material . . . concerning other subjects'. Some years ago Jim Campbell (1990) warned of the loss of a 'broad and balanced curriculum' if core subjects were overemphasised. More books are now being published on history with texts suitable for six- and nine-year-olds to read themselves. Some publishers are providing taped history stories for younger children to listen to while they look at pictures of the same story. Therefore, this should help teachers have the confidence to introduce at least some of the eight units into

integrated work already being done, and to use historical materials for teaching purposes.

The well-known topic approach has been the vehicle for historical material for the last twenty years. There is no need to prove, here, that history was seldom treated well in this context, as many leading authorities have shown this (DES, 1989; Thomas, 1992). The Discussion Paper of 1992 (Alexander *et al.*) states 'certain subjects now in the National Curriculum, notably art, history and geography, have been, and remain, particularly vulnerable' and they are cited as 'perennial losers'. Not only teachers want to link history to other subject areas of the curriculum, but the 1994 Dearing Proposals also require consideration of the perspectives (PESCR formula) (see Figure 21 opposite). Cross-curricular themes should still be considered but are not mentioned in the Dearing Proposals. *The National Curriculum in Key Stages 1 and 2* (National Curriculum Council, 1993) favours the 'subject-based approach' and questions the 'seamlessness' of knowledge.

It is difficult to give specific advice as to which units to study, and how and where they should be studied as integrated with other areas, or as discrete subjects. Not only is one chapter insufficient for this, but types of school over the national scene are 'extremely diverse' (Alexander *et al.*, 1992); some have under ten pupils and some have eight hundred, though the norm is about two hundred. In addition, schools vary in location, clientele, teachers and school policy. As a result, I believe that the decision about whether units should be integrated or discrete should be left to schools. Hilary Cooper (1992) favours integration as it stands, but suggests that history should really have been a core subject with mathematics, language and science and so the basis of much of the curriculum. In Key Stage 1 she thinks that local and family history forming the main ingredient are natural integrators. She suggests a strong history focus, or 'history-driven' topic for one term (as does the Welsh Final Order). This could come from unit 3, 'Victorian Britain', or unit 4, 'Britain since 1930', in Years 3 and 4. The source evidence for these units, being in readable English, are more easily found and used by teachers. Thus Victorian census returns are to be found in local record offices and can be linked to the streets in which the children actually live. Census returns can be used for mathematical problem solving and many other subjects including local geography. Extension study A, 'Ships and seafarers' or 'Domestic life, families and childhood' (favourite choices) and Extension study B, local studies, also relate easily to number, geography, technology, art, music, drama and language. Using Hilary Cooper's ideas, four out of eight units are easily used as integrators. These four units could constitute the main topic in the four years and the other four could be taught as discrete subjects. She also suggested studying 'Victorian Britain' as a whole-school topic, presumably for a term. Whole-school themes present problems of organisation and use of the manageable resources for the particular topic with the varying ages of seven- to eleven-year-olds. Checks with cross-curricular themes and perspectives should be made, though it is not a good thing to distort the unit to introduce them.

There have been various suggestions about how much time should be spent on history. The Dearing Proposals specify thirty-six hours for Key Stage 1 and forty-five for Key Stage 2. In addition, the 'free' day (20 per cent of the week) could be used (Dearing Report, January 1994, p. 33, section 4.20). Lengthening the school day or term might appear to create more time but

certainly not quality teaching and learning. As long as history is assessed at age seven and age eleven, the *amount* of time is not important, nor is the method of organisation. The quality of work is the important factor.

Another decision has to be made about links between units in planning their order. The 1991 National Curriculum Council Non-Statutory Guidance in diagram C 2 writes of the danger of fragmentation – 'breaking them [the units] down into pieces of content and reassembling them destroys their focus and cannot be recommended'. This presents problems in view of teachers' apprehensions about too much content. Many publishers and local education authorities are recommending treating the Extension study A of themes over a long period of time as part of the core units. For example, 'Ships and seafarers' could be studied with unit 2 'Life in Tudor Times' This poses a problem for the coordinator to relate the separate parts of the long unit to each other *along a time-line* in Year 5. Will the coordinator do it him/herself ? Will he/she be teaching Year 5 each year? The coordinator will have to find out from special files built up by pupils over the three years how each part of the unit has been studied, if studied at all! Many schools are avoiding this problem by treating the A study as a theme in itself for a term (see 'Houses and places of worship' in Chapter 7, p. 56). This is the most historical treatment and reinforces children's concept of time, as use of a time-line is essential. The other units can be 'revisited' if only for a short time. The 1991 Guidance gives examples of how units should be linked according to time ('The Maya', and 'Life in Tudor Times') or theme ('Victorian Britain' and 'Domestic life, families and childhood'). They do not favour three core units being studied in one year. Also Key Stage 1 could be linked to Key Stage 2 by studying Extension study B (local unit) in term one of Year 3, and Key Stage 2 to Key Stage 3 by studying 'Houses and places of worship' in term 3 of Year 6 to link to 'Medieval realms' in Key Stage 3 in Year 7. However, each school with this organisation also has the problem of some children staying in the same year again and joining a group coming up the school. Children may also leave the school to live in another location. But concern should not be felt if a unit or two are omitted from a child's experience. Children should have collected enough historical skills to be assessed sufficiently well. Again quality of work rather than amount of content is the most important factor.

The linchpin of history, or any other subject, in the whole curriculum, is the subject coordinator. This was an idea long before the emergence of the National Curriculum. In *Better Schools* (DES, 1985) the then Secretary of State for Education, Sir Keith Joseph, wrote of the need for such a person if schools were to be 'better' – 'older primary pupils . . . need to benefit from more expertise than a single class teacher can reasonably be expected to possess' – 'to teach it to classes other than his own'. Unfortunately *Better Schools* believes that schools have enough expertise in humanities and aesthetic subjects and that mathematics, science and music need more help. By the time the History Final Order was published in 1991, teachers needed as much help in the humanities and more help than in mathematics!

In the meantime, *The Teaching of History and Geography* (DES, 1989) showed that topic work had not been beneficial to the humanities subjects. Schools began to appoint coordinators, but they were too often already responsible for a core subject as well, and could not honestly undertake yet another subject to master in depth. At best they were responsible for geography as well as history, they were short of money for resources and in some cases older/more established colleagues and the headteachers would not support their efforts to make real alterations. Humanities coordinators could become a name, not a function. The National Curriculum has helped in this respect. The Discussion Paper (Alexander *et al.*, 1992) puts great emphasis on the need for strong

coordinators if standards are to be improved. Not only should a history coordinator plan history in the whole curriculum and collect resources for the whole school but help teachers with reading, techniques and assessment. The Paper says that there is a need for history specialists in Key Stage 1, but this estimate grows to sixty per cent of staff time in Years 5 and 6. Teachers do not need to have degrees in history but can make themselves into specialists through their own reading, by attending in-service courses and by their own enthusiasm. They should start by knowing the meaning of history as a discipline (Noble, 1986; Nichol, 1981). The Discussion Paper suggests joining small schools into clusters to gain from one specialist. A coordinator is needed to:

- provide knowledge;
- ensure continuity between Key Stages 1, 2 and 3;
- suggest ways of getting progression in skills (for example, setting more difficult work and activities);
- explain the meaning of details of the National Curriculum;
- collect resources;
- help teachers with historical techniques;
- teach history to many classes.

Recent publications may assist in the work of the coordinator, and they include: Hilary Cooper's *The Teaching of History* (1992), Julie Davies' chapter in *Beyond the Core Curriculum* (Harrison, 1994) and Jim Campbell's *Developing the Primary School Curriculum* (1985). At the present moment decisions about history in the whole curriculum are dependent on the next few years in each school for any generalisations to be made. Nevertheless the coordinator is a key and essential figure.

Resources

This book's scope covers how to approach the National Curriculum and its content coverage of eight units in the limited time for preparation and classroom encounter. Methods of teaching history remain the same as they were before the National Curriculum. Although the statutory nature of the Final Order (1991) has led to many useful publications, resources used in the past may be just as effective. Museum visits and publications, radio and television programmes and publications are also being geared to the National Curriculum with excellent results. Perhaps the most valuable resource for the teacher is *time* but this is not for sale! Therefore study units should be selected to use resources already in the school. In this chapter, I will concentrate on four particularly valuable resources, and provide lists of other highly selected resources in the appendices. Two of my chosen resources are pictures and buildings for children to visit. The other two are more unusual – music and a specific old school building.

In selecting any resources, certain criteria should be observed. Reviews in *Primary History, Junior Education* and the *Times Educational Supplement* should also be considered. The first criterion is that the resources should be accurate and contain up-to-date history in fact, date and point of view. This also applies to illustrations of all kinds. The second criterion is that publications should lead teachers and children to find out more, to read more books and to be more observant on visits outside the school. They should lead to discussion and historical thinking. Beware of slavishly following books which profess to provide 'all you need to know'. This also applies to radio and television programmes. Activities for children should be historical ones, not colouring in photocopiable sheets to occupy time. It is wise not to use the same publisher for all years of Key Stage 2. A third criterion is to look at the language of books to make sure that they are suitable for the reading age of the class concerned. This is naturally more difficult in a mixed-age class. A fourth criterion is that resources should be easy to handle, collect and store. Activities should not depend upon lost parts of packs. Lastly, all resources should cut down on teachers' work, not increase it. In this connection, there are two gaps in resources at present. One is a book of photocopiable sheets giving short extracts from well-known historical and literary sources to illustrate the National Curriculum units. The other is a pack of audio cassettes of historical stories 'beyond living memory' for Key Stage 1. These would be time-saving additions to resources for primary teachers.

Many references are made throughout this book to specific resources for particular units, especially for Key Stage 1 in Chapter 5. Many more could have been included, but these tend to be unobtainable after a certain number of years. If more details are needed of perennially useful resources, teachers are advised to refer to my previous books, detailed in the bibliography.

PICTURES

Pictures are the most attractive source of evidence in the primary school. They provide evidence for the Attainment Target; they give knowledge; they are a primary source for how one age depicts another age; and they can supply different evidence for the same part of the past. 'Pictures' is a general term used for illustrations from cave-paintings and old maps to colour photographs, television programmes and video cassettes. They can be used for whole class lessons, with the teacher explaining them, and for many class activities throughout the five-to-eleven age range, but are particularly useful with four- to eight-year-olds and older non-readers. Therefore I shall concentrate on pictures for Key Stage 1, though plenty of material is now being published for all the eight units in Key Stage 2.

Teachers should be selective about the offerings made to them by publishers. There are obvious and more unusual places to find pictures. However, in pupils' history texts there are many types of pictures. The advent of the technological revolution has enabled publishers to produce clear pictures from many sources, many of which are in colour. Before about 1970, publishers employed one artist to create all the pictures for a series of books; R. J. Unstead's 'Looking at History' series (A and C Black) and the early books in Longman's 'Then and There' series are examples. By 1990, several artists were often employed for each book, enabling children to look at different interpretations, photographs, aerial photographs, contemporary paintings, cartoons, parts of old maps, brass rubbings, stained-glass windows and embroidered pictures (the Bayeux Tapestry). Macmillan published their 'History Class Pictures of British History' as posters for classrooms for many years and Pictorial Charts Educational Trust is now producing high quality charts/posters/packs for Key Stages 1 and 2 units with concise teachers' notes written by specialists. Other poster-type pictures are sold by museums and art galleries,

and large coloured pictures are an essential part of the new packs published by Longman, Collins and Ginn. *Junior Education* also publishes large pictures in relation to the theme of the month. Art galleries, notably the National Portrait Gallery in London, sell postcards of their exhibits. Children like buying these themselves, and they are well used for sequencing exercises. Some pictures are to be found in archive offices and cathedral libraries, especially examples of medieval life from manuscripts. Television programmes often use pictures inaccessible to teachers which are repeated in their teachers' and pupils' notes.

Finding a variety of pictures is only the beginning. Picture-reading should be taught to children from the age of four. To do this, teachers should get to know as much as possible about each picture. Dependent upon their size, pictures can be used for an oral lesson by the teacher for the whole class, by children individually or in groups, and for display, either as they stand or attached to time-lines. Children should be helped to look closely at one picture, if necessary using a magnifying glass. Then discussion with the teacher, or in groups for older children, should take place, based around such questions as: Who are the people in the picture? What is happening in the picture? Try to sequence the events in this story – why is the story important? What are the names of the clothes, furniture and buildings used at the time of the picture? Do you think that the artist has given us a true story of the past in this picture? Nineteenth-century artists depicting seventeenth-century events of the past provide a golden opportunity for older juniors to see how one century depicts another century. In 1859 J. Petty depicted the Duke of Monmouth grovelling for his life with King James II, but this incident never took place. Activities from this close observation might include tape-recording the story of the picture, writing it down or role-playing the story. If a large poster from the

National Portrait Gallery (for example 'The Family of Thomas More') can be supported by a postcard of the same picture (one between two children), much individual work can be done following the class discussion.

Research into picture-reading in history by Susan Lynn has been summarised in Chapter 3, but in addition Stuart Marriott ascertained what sort of pictures generally were liked, and therefore studied closely by children of age four, seven and ten. He showed a group of children eight illustrations from children's story books and asked which they liked best. They preferred pictures to be in colour, large enough to see the detail and to reflect and extend the meaning of the text. He inferred from this that certain artists from the 'Ladybird' series of stories could help children to read more quickly and fluently (Marriott, 1992).

The colour of clothes and buildings is a specialised topic, and the knowledge of a costume expert is often needed to gain authenticity. For instance, Susan Morris warns that colour slides and pictures on television programmes show brighter than natural colour (Morris, 1989); and the highly coloured clothes of people shown in stained-glass windows, in some medieval manuscripts and in most children's books are misleading. The dyes for these colours were expensive and most people wore brown, grey or beige clothes, as these colours occurred naturally in the fibres. This situation remained until well into the seventeenth century. Thomas Brerewood, glove-maker and mayor of Chester in Elizabeth I's reign, was allowed to wear purple and red, and to have fur on his clothes when he became sufficiently wealthy and important to have the 'status' to wear them. Apprentices in the Tudor period all wore royal blue to distinguish them in the streets and to ensure their good behaviour. Therefore children should not be allowed to use any colour they fancy on their 'photocopiable sheets' found in many of the new resources.

If 'seeing is believing', then it goes without saying that pictures in great variety are natural resources for history in the primary school. Learning how to know about the past through pictures as well as through the written and spoken word is an education in itself for adults of the future.

BUILDINGS

Buildings of all types figure extensively in the National Curriculum. They illustrate all the study units in varying degrees according to locality. They are especially useful as sources of children's observation and activity in core units 2, 3 and 4 ('Life in Tudor Times', 'Victorian Britain' and 'Britain since 1930'). They also form a large part of extension study B on various types of local history. Two themes in 'Houses and places of worship' (1991 Non-Statutory Guidance F3) are the technology of building and buildings as a reflection of social life. Therefore all the units refer to buildings in different ways, and teachers are left to work out the meaning of this advice.

My advice is that it is always better to study specific buildings in your own locality.

Most of the buildings to illustrate the eight units are situated in Britain. Those in Greece, Egypt and Mexico have to be studied through pictures and models in museums. Therefore teachers should know an outline of the historical influences affecting building as a background to specific units. The Romans brought ideas of their traditional buildings in the early first century (Hadrian's Wall, town walls and villas) but their departure about 400 AD was followed by Saxon invaders who fought but did not build in an unsettled and ravaged country. The exception was

Figure 22   A Medieval Merchant's House, Southampton

Death of 1348 decreased population and therefore the means and need to build. The fifteenth-century Wars of the Roses led to more demolition rather than rebuilding. Prosperity did not return until the sixteenth and seventeenth centuries with the initial stability of the Tudor monarchy. Some of the greatest houses were built during the period 1500–1640; for instance, Hampton Court Palace and Hardwick Hall. Henry VIII's devastation of the monasteries and their extensive lands led to new building by the nobility enriched by monastic spoils. W. G. Hoskins (1976) aptly names this period of 1500–47 as 'The Age of Plunder'. The English Civil War of 1642–6 saw a decrease in building and the ruin of many fine houses. But in the eighteenth century and the Victorian period a revival of building took place. Many of our fine municipal buildings still standing are witness to this growth. Famous travellers from the seventeenth century onwards tell us in their diaries of how the buildings of England appeared to them. John Leland, William Camden, Celia Fiennes and Daniel Defoe are some of these travellers. These varying views of the past of one age by another, and different views of the same buildings satisfy the needs of the Attainment Target.

Types of buildings for study may be divided into four categories. These are: houses, churches and cathedrals, public buildings and farm buildings. There are 'listed buildings' decided by the Department of the Environment to be of 'special architectural or historical interest' and known as Grade I or II. It is useful for older children to compare one of these with a less prestigious one in the same locality. All sorts of buildings lend themselves to cross-curricular links, and basic questions may be asked of all of them (see Appendix 2). The choice of buildings should reflect the difficulty of understanding in the five-to-eleven age range. Thus, a small compact building, such as a worker's cottage, a pig sty or a windmill, is better for younger children, whereas nine- or ten-year-olds can understand the remains of a Roman villa or the great hall of Hampton

the rulers of Kent who obeyed the new invaders and therefore had money and time to build. It was not until King Alfred's time, about 900 AD, when the country became more settled that 'burhs' (towns) were built in wood and churches and monasteries were erected. London, pre-eminent amongst British towns, began to have more permanent buildings. The Norman Conquest of 1066 really started the medieval flowering of buildings, this time in stone, which means that some can be visited today (for example, the White Tower in the Tower of London). William I built castles in many parts of the country for defensive purposes. The stability given by Norman domination and the accumulation of wealth and trade encouraged more building of domestic houses as well as public buildings, such as guild halls. The Black

Court Palace.

Domestic houses are the greatest sign of prosperity from about 1500 onwards. The age of Adam and Regency houses (c.1700–1850) can only be included in the Extension study A, 'Houses and places of worship', or the Extension study B in one of the types of local study. But there are plenty of standing miracles in the great houses built by wealthy courtiers, in smaller black and white Tudor houses and various styles of Victorian and twentieth-century buildings. Stone arches, villas, castles and abbeys are also 'domestic houses'.

Churches and cathedrals are all-purpose buildings which were used throughout the ages, altered and restored, though their essential structure may represent one particular period. One church or one house studied in depth makes a good line of development leading to a better understanding of chronology. 'Churches and places of worship' caters for this in Extension study A.

Houses and churches are already well used by teachers, but public buildings are often overlooked on account of inaccessibility. Town children have greater opportunity to look at Victorian Gothic town halls, hotels built in the nineteenth century, cinemas, shopping centres, art galleries and museums, libraries, old mills, old concert halls and old school buildings (see Sevington School in this chapter). London and the northern industrial towns have examples of these buildings in profusion.

The pyramids (c.2000 BC) may well form a study for 'Ancient Egypt' as one of the Extension study C non-European choices. This would have to be vicarious viewing. The technology of building a pyramid is well illustrated in David Macaulays' *Pyramid* (1975), one of a series of architectural picture books published by Collins.

Buildings in the country are less obvious, but the structure of them is usually simple and there are various sizes suitable for all ages of children to study. The monks were the first great farmers and introduced new farming techniques in the twelfth and thirteenth centuries. Monastic barns are the biggest legacy of the Middle Ages. The next big development in farming was during the sixteenth century when more arable land was enclosed for sheep farming. This led to wealthier farmers building stone barns rather than more perishable wooden ones. More farm buildings will be found today in areas of mixed farming rather than in solely arable or pasture farming areas. This may account for the number in your locality. They are located in hamlets or villages. Other farm buildings include: cow sheds, stables, granaries, cart sheds, dovecots, windmills and oast houses (in Kent). 'Food and farming' over 'a long period of time' from 1066 to the present day (Extension study A) could include buildings as one element of this 'line of development'.

Throughout history, building materials have changed according to local geology and means of transport, varying from soil to wood, thatch, brick, stone and more recently concrete. This provides a good link with technology, and children should be encouraged to make simple models, even if the materials cannot be identical. Buildings can be studied from pictures and videos, but whenever possible a visit should be the centre of the work.

The following section on music as a source of information for History in the National Curriculum has been written by Penelope Harnett of the University of the West of England.

MUSIC

The National Curriculum in History includes music as a source of information for the study of history, and the purpose of this account is to explore some of the ways in which music can be used to enrich children's historical understanding. Listening to music, singing and performing can all extend children's awareness of particular periods in the past by looking at how people used music in their leisure time, as well as at work or in their worship. A study of lyrics of songs and nursery rhymes can provide information about ways of life in the past. Different versions of rhymes and songs provide children with examples of how variations occur as lyrics are passed down through word of mouth. Opportunities for investigating ideas about change and continuity can arise from studying the different instruments which were played and noting how these instruments have developed over time. Musicals offer children different interpretations of history which can be investigated and discussed.

Listening to and performing music provides children with opportunities to identify more closely with people in the past and to become aware of their different interests and values. From earliest times music has played a significant role in people's leisure activities. Wall paintings and mosaics reveal Egyptian and Roman musicians playing different instruments, performing at banquets and playing accompaniments for dances. Musicians have attempted to reconstruct the sounds of music from these periods, and tapes are available which provide examples of such music which could be used by children as a stimulus for their own performances.

The folk tradition continued to develop in Anglo-Saxon and Viking times. Minstrels and storytellers sang and told their stories to the accompaniment of instruments such as rebecs (a precursor of the violin with three strings), harps and lyres, drums and shawms (double set of reeds). This folk music presents a contrast with the developing liturgical music in the monasteries, nunneries and churches at the time.

Children can listen to and sing songs and madrigals which date back to Tudor times. There is also a wide variety of music available which children can listen to and perform and use as accompaniments for dances and other entertainments. In their series, *Music from the Past* (Longman, 1986 [Victorian], 1987 [Tudor and Stuart] 1988 [Medieval]), Alison and Michael Bagenal provide many examples of songs and music to play, together with a great deal of background information. Their books suggest different scenarios where music can be incorporated, and include ideas for costumes and props, etc.

Popular music in Victorian times includes music hall songs, parlour songs and songs from light operas by composers such as Gilbert and Sullivan. Band music was also popular, as the number of bandstands in Victorian parks and on promenades bears testimony. This music provides a contrast with the music of grand operas and the large symphony orchestras, which children might like to discuss.

For more recent times, children could ask their parents and grandparents what music they enjoyed when they were at school. Comparisons between different oral accounts could be made and children could add their own opinions after listening to the music. Children might also like to learn some of the dances associated with the music, for example, the jive, the twist, rock 'n' roll, the jitterbug. Music could also act as a stimulus to an investigation on fashion and youth culture, particularly since the last war.

Music was, and still is, an important feature in certain working environments. Ancient Greeks had worksongs to accompany such tasks as threshing barley, treading grapes, spinning wool, making rope and drawing water. Some of this tradition continues in Mediterranean countries today. Children might like to devise their own songs to accompany different tasks. Children should learn some of the sea shanties which were sung as sailors turned the capstan or pulled on the rigging, often as a call and response activity as they worked in time to the call of the shantyman. Learning some of the cries of street traders, such as 'Hot cross buns', 'Who'll buy my lavender, fresh lavender'; 'Old chairs to mend, old chairs to mend', can help children become more aware of changes in town life. They could contrast the sounds of different traders in the past with the roar of modern-day traffic, with perhaps the tune of the ice-cream van in the background.

Many nursery rhymes provide opportunities for raising questions about life in the past. Questions which might be raised could include: Why did Jack and Jill have to go to the well to fetch water? Who was the muffin man and what was he selling? Why did Polly Flinders get so dirty? What were cinders? In raising questions, children are starting the process of historical enquiry. Differences and similarities in lifestyles can be noted and children encouraged to suggest some reasons for the observations which they have made.

The origins of many well-known nursery rhymes are interesting to investigate. For example, it is thought that 'Humpty Dumpty' might refer to the downfall of Charles I and 'Baa Baa Black Sheep' to the prosperous wool trade in the Middle Ages. Some songs and rhymes can be linked to actual places and events, for example, 'London's burning' and 'London Bridge is falling down' to the Great Fire of 1666; 'Yankee Doodle' to the American War of Independence and 'Colon Man' is linked with the building of the Panama Canal. Older children might like to trace the origins of well-known rhymes and songs. Many rhymes present a curious mix of fact and fiction, and children could be encouraged to suggest what parts might have been true or to devise their own interpretations of well-known rhymes.

Playground games and rhymes provide an example that the oral tradition still flourishes today. Current rhymes and games, played by children today, can be contrasted with those played by their parents and grandparents. Suggestions can be made as to why there might be differences in some of the lines. Such comparisons provide opportunities for developing children's awareness of oral traditions and of how these traditions are passed on by word of mouth from one generation to the next. As children participate in singing games and dances, they are continuing and adding to childhood traditions. The Opies (1985) have traced regional variations of different rhymes and also noted how words can be changed by events.

Songs and rhymes can also reflect the particular beliefs and feelings of a period of the time. Propaganda songs from World War I convey a sense of optimism and cheerfulness. Victorian hymns reflect the supremacy of Empire ('From Greenland's Icy Mountains') and notions of social order ('All Things Bright and Beautiful'). Older children might like to question some of these values and contrast them with those of today.

Songs which link with particular seasons and celebrations can help develop children's awareness of seasonal change and of the passage of time, for example, 'Christmas is coming and the goose is getting fat', 'Please to remember the fifth of November', 'Hot Cross Buns', 'Diwali Avi' (all published in *Tinderbox* – see 'Music' in Appendix 2). *A Musical Calendar of Festivals* – see 'Music' in Appendix 2 – has a range of songs and rhymes which can be associated with different times of the year. Some carols, such as the 'Boar's Head Carol', also record how Christmas has been celebrated in the past.

Sequencing skills, which are important for acquiring a sense of historical chronology can be developed through songs: 'O soldier soldier won't you marry me?' can be used as a dressing sequence and 'Dashing away with the smoothing iron' as a sequence for washing clothes. 'When Susie was a Baby, a Baby Susie was' describes the different stages of life, culminating with the appearance of the skeleton which goes 'creak,

creak'. These songs can help children engage with the concept of time passing and also enable them to use some of the language associated with the passage of time.

Investigating the ways in which music has been made can help children recognise some of the continuous threads which link the basic design of musical instruments. For example, electronic keyboards and synthesisers have their roots in the xylophone family; and valved and reed instruments have developed from simple pipes. Children can be encouraged to make their own instruments) which could help them to appreciate the technology of their construction and the difficulties which earlier instrument makers were

able to overcome. A musical time-line would be an interesting way for children to record the changes in instrument design.

Musicals such as *Oliver* and *Mary Poppins* are an interesting way to explore different interpretations of history, linking with the Attainment Target. Children could raise questions such as whether these musicals are authentic reconstructions and on what historical evidence they are based.

The following account of Sevington School, an authentic Victorian school in Chippenham, Wiltshire has been written by Jo Lawrie.

SEVINGTON SCHOOL

Situated in a tiny hamlet near Chippenham, Wiltshire, is a delightful, authentic Victorian school which re-opened in November 1991, still almost unchanged after an eighty-year closure. A group of local teachers, convinced of the unique educational value of the resource, set up 'The Sevington School Project' to administer the premises as a non-profit making, charitable trust. Now present-day schoolchildren can go there for a day's experience of nineteenth-century life.

Pupils, in groups of no more than thirty-five, can have sole use of the premises for four hours. In order to maximise the potential of the day, their teachers will already have been on an in-service visit and will have received a complimentary folder of preparatory material.

Resource materials and specialist publications are on offer to encourage stimulating schoolwork, before and after the visit. The class teacher can use registers, census returns and old maps to reinforce National Curriculum skills and concepts. Photographs, biographical detail and the memories of the last surviving pupil add the human interest which brings history to life.

The session is run by an experienced curriculum support teacher who adopts the role of Miss Squire, erstwhile headmistress of the school. Everyone is in costume and in role for the whole time and this makes for an unforgettable firsthand experience. This is enriched by the use of such unfamiliar items as dip-in ink pens, copybooks and thimbles for sewing. At break there are hoops, hobby horses and a whip and top to play with. The more unusual lessons include drill, verbal gymnastics and geometric drawing. Great attention is paid to moral and religious education as well as to personal cleanliness and good deportment. Lessons are set in the context of the Victorian social order with occasional visits from the local squirearchy (adults unknown to the children who might appear as the rector or the patron, Sir Aydley Neeld).

The schoolroom has an impressive nineteenth-century atmosphere, and both it and the schoolhouse are as authentic as is practicable, including oil lamps and a functioning kitchen range. Further attention to detail includes a ticking clock, carbolic soap in the kitchen, and original

Figure 23 Sevington School, Chippenham, Wiltshire – an authentic Victorian school

Figure 24 Children experiencing a nineteenth-century day at Sevington School

Victorian coins. In the vicinity are a pump, a wash-house and a defunct earth closet. The garden is being restored as it might have looked in the nineteenth century, ultimately to be used as an additional resource offering culinary and medicinal herbs and vegetables. Ingredients for typical country recipes like elderflower cordial will likewise illustrate the self-sufficiency typical of the period. Indeed, an authentic lunch is already part of the day and ingenious visitors have researched and prepared such delights as ginger beer, cornish pasties and even a hot potato (used *en route* for warming hands and then placed by the stove on arrival). Thus pupils not only experience the routine, content and discipline of a Victorian schoolday; there is also the chance to

learn about everyday rural domestic economy and to encounter a variety of types of evidence, not least the building itself.

Having already absorbed the idea of the 'history detective', who finds out about the past using clues, Key Stage 1 pupils can now put this into practice. They can do observational drawings, examine artefacts and then use them for their intended purpose in a Victorian setting. They can look at original garments and experience a Victorian washday, using a posser, a scrubbing board and dolly pegs. They can relish the pleasure of polishing a brass candlestick to shining perfection. Key Stage 2 pupils are capable of a more sophisticated grasp of concepts and are faced with more difficult activities which will satisfy the more rigorous demands of the Attainment Target. Once again, it is the first-hand contact with authentic artefacts which will interest and then inform. One such experience is to discover how an oil lamp works, watch it being filled through an enamel funnel, smell the paraffin and trim the wick before it is lit with a taper. Alternatively, wielding a carpet beater can lead to an appreciation of the benefits of labour-saving devices far more readily than any amount of talking or reading.

There are innumerable opportunities for such potentially cross-curricular activities. Once back at school, the teacher can expand on information and pointers offered during the role-play and encourage pupils' ability to make deductions and comparisons, to sequence and to understand the process of change and continuity.

Figure 25   Sevington School: using an abacus

Clues to the past abound but it is the whole environment which inspires. The first sight of the school and its surroundings, as the children walk from the edge of the village, is the real start of their Sevington experience: particularly so if they are already in costume and in role. Some borrow the available pinafores and 'granddad' shirts but many research and provide their own costumes. This, in itself, offers a valuable learning experience evinced by the ringlets, lace-up boots, pinned-on handkerchiefs and fine details such as torn-up rags for bandages. The 'scholars' have names such as 'Ernest' or 'Ada', often taken from the original registers. Some children found out a great deal about their 'character', as shown in the role-play. They may know the names of the rest of their 'family' and details of the father's job as well as their route to school, perhaps along the lime

walk from the next village. Their involvement in the minutiae of nineteenth-century life is often revealed by the ingenious excuses they offer to explain lateness or the absence of their 'school' penny.

The children are always fascinated by the separation of the boys and girls in both the seating arrangements and at playtime. A very sexist moral homily and some differing lessons reinforce this, and again it provides food for subsequent discussion. During the school day, a few girls might be withdrawn to learn household skills, in readiness for a probable career as a domestic servant. They might learn to make a rag rug or to prepare a soup with stock, dried peas and fresh vegetables. When the peelings are despatched to the pig, we are reminded to 'Waste not want not'. Such moral interjections are

Figure 26   Sevington School: a visiting pupil using a flat iron

a regular feature of the day: they illustrate attitudes implicit in nineteenth-century life and often introduce unfamiliar vocabulary, as in the case of 'Procrastination is the thief of time'. Meanwhile, the boys could be hearing about their own employment prospects: farmwork, apprenticeship or even a 'white-collar' job. The phrase can be clearly exemplified at a later point in the day when an attempt is made to fix a starched white-collar onto a shirt using a collar stud. Polishing a pair of leather-soled boots, examining a cobbler's last and looking at a contemporary household budget (with 3/6d for boots deducted from the weekly income of 10/-) are equally painless ways of fulfilling the requirements of the National Curriculum.

After the presentation of attendance medals and certificates of merit for the attainment of Standard Five, there is a Victorian prayer and the class is dismissed. The pupils are now ready to make their way back along the village street to their waiting 'carriage'. The monitors follow close behind after cleaning the slates and filling the inkwells. Sadly the day must end with the 'scholars'' return to the twentieth century. However, letters and drawings subsequently sent to 'Miss Squire' serve to illustrate the quality of the work evoked by this memorable journey into the past.

> Mon 1st Feb
> Sevington School
> We went to Sevington School because we are talking about Victorian times. We had bring a Victorian lunch I brought an apple, cheese sand wich, cake, pork pie and an egg. The girls made some home made lemonade I found it to Sharp and Soup that was all right! We played with the wooden hoops and worked in the class room we played with the Victorian toys, the boys shined some boots and Mrs. lawrie gave us some liquid. And we wrote on slates and we got some thing from the shop we were not allowed to spend more then 1 pound we could get a Sugar mouse, pad, post card, mug, Flick Book, peg doll and a book.
>
> Benjamin aged 8

Figure 27 Sevington School: Benjamin's account of his visit

TEN

Assessment and recording

By 1993, assessment became the 'problem child' of the National Curriculum in both primary and secondary schools. Unlike the core subjects, history is to be assessed by teachers with no official Standard Assessment Tasks (SATs) involved. As I write, teachers and groups of teachers are being invited by Sir Ron Dearing, the 'top man' at the new School Curriculum and Assessment Authority (SCAA), to express their views mainly about assessment, though this also involves the content of the National Curriculum in all subjects. Decisions will have been made by the time this book is published, therefore my help to teachers can only consist of 'hunches' and will have to be reviewed.

Assessment is closely linked with the Attainment Target in history, detailed in Chapter 4 of this book. Statements of attainment in the Final Order (1991) have been replaced by 'Level descriptions'. The first five levels relate to Key Stages 1 and 2 (1994 Dearing Proposals, p. 14). Therefore the Attainment Target is concerned with knowledge of the past and how children use a multitude of sources to understand the past.

The object of assessment is to tell children, parents, governors and both primary and secondary schools the standard reached by each child and to suggest how this can be improved. Too detailed assessment and recording can be time-consuming, confusing and tiring for all

concerned. In history, the main object is to ascertain whether, by the age of eleven, a child has a great interest in history, a moderate one or not much at all. Therefore to me it is 'degrees of interest', not five level descriptions that should be loosely considered for Years 5–11. To do this with confidence, teachers should know some history, at least the units they teach, be readers of history, be aware of historical skills and concepts, and instil their own enthusiasm into the children by discussion and by providing interesting activities. Teachers need time to read and attend in-service courses and so gradually make their chosen units 'interesting, exciting and enjoyable', 'bringing history to life', in the words of the Final Report of the Working Party (July, 1990). Even if 'degrees of interest' are substituted for the five levels of achievement and level descriptions are only noted, adult assistance is needed in the classroom, particularly at Key Stage 1. A multitude of resources is also needed for young children to use as activities. Tasks should be set with a view to children making progress in historical understanding. Schools Examination and Assessment Council (SEAC) material for Key Stage 1 are very useful in this respect and will be discussed later. The Nuffield Primary History Project, based at the University of Exeter, believes in children knowing about the Attainment Target and what teachers are looking for in their work.

KEY STAGE 1

Learning history in Key Stage 1 is one of the most novel ideas of the National Curriculum (see Chapter 5). Assessing it in the summer of 1993 at age seven was an even more revolutionary practice. Most infant teachers have enjoyed teaching about the past, particularly 'since 1945', and have welcomed the help given to them by two publications from SEAC. The first is a pack sent to schools in January 1993 as preparation for the assessment in the summer term of 1993. It is called *Standard Assessment Tasks* and was trialled by NFER staff (National Foundation of Educational Research). The second – *Children's Work Assessed: Geography and History* – was published in May 1993. Both publications will now be discussed.

The SAT guide is divided into four parts, showing teachers how to use stories, photographs, objects and time-lines to accomplish the Attainment Target. Teachers are encouraged to *tell* stories to children 'in their own words', reading a story being a less acceptable form of teaching. *How* to tell history stories is not considered, but help is given in a minority of method books (Blyth, 1990; Colwell, 1991). Telling historical stories as distinct from other stories has its own pitfalls which can be overcome with practice. It is a pity that no stories from the medieval period have been selected as examples, such as Robert the Bruce and Dick Whittington, since they are omitted from Key Stage 2. The trialling of myths and legends by NFER found that infants could not distinguish between real and fictional characters or historical facts and points of view. The stories supply material for knowledge in the Attainment Target. Using historical sources is catered for in the booklets (in the SEAC packs) on photographs and objects. The seven photographs in the booklet, ranging from 1900 to 1955, are concerned with home, shops, children and familiar everyday happenings. Much useful support for this work can be found in the *Starting History* series from Scholastic (Hughes and Cox, 1991), which

provides large pictures on similar topics. It is a pity that other pictures as sources are not used to understand 'life before living memory' (see Chapter 9 for examples of such pictures). Objects of familiar ways of life since 1945 should be collected to form a developing school museum. It is more difficult to provide objects before 1900 unless they are replicas. For example, seven-year-olds should be helped to see the difference between a hat of the seventeenth century and one of the nineteenth century, rather than all comparisons being made with the late-twentieth century, which is familiar to them.

The Attainment Target is catered for in the booklet entitled *Change in History*. The activities recommended are all related to children making time-lines with their own pictures and writing. Examples of children's work are provided to show how they place familiar objects in chronological order, describe changes over a period of time, give reasons for a historical event or development and identify differences between times in the past. All the topics covered in the four booklets lead to reaching different levels of the Attainment Target. The *Teachers' Handbook* leads teachers through the four activities. The whole pack is very detailed, thorough and time-consuming but, as it emphasises, can only be undertaken when children are ready for it from previous similar work. Therefore, these materials should be studied and used by teachers as they stand, or as examples to make their own tests at different stages of the infant school and not all in the last four weeks of the summer term. On the whole, the 'Optional SAT materials have been well-received' ('Relics of the Iron Age', TES, 19 March, 1993).

Children's Work Assessed – Geography and History (SEAC, 1993 and NFER, Nelson) shows written work of seven-year-olds and transcriptions of taped discussions with their teachers. The samples were taken from schools in West Yorkshire, Greater Manchester, Kent, Suffolk, Dorset and

Wales. Therefore, they represent a wide geographical spread. In each individual case, comments are made on the child's work in relation to the Attainment Target and ways forward suggested to help that child to progress. 'Everyday life in the past', 'Beyond Living memory', 'Life since World War II', 'Famous men and women' and 'Family history' were tested by different activities. The conclusions reached were optimistic and show that, in history, the standard of reasoning, use of sources and historical discussion is high in seven-year-olds and the writing is good. This booklet also shows that work can be organised in class, group, paired and individual activities.

These two SEAC publications should be considered as advice rather than a rigid system. Teachers should use them or their own similar tests when particular children are ready for them any time during the two years. All children in a class will not work through all the activities. In *Standard Assessment Tasks* choice should be made between photographs and objects. If a loose record is kept over the two years, a general assessment could be made in the last term. This could be an interest in the past by the letter 'H' and possibly the number '1' (H1) on the general record card as information for the teacher of Year 3 in the junior school. Degree of interest is more easily gauged than level descriptions. Most seven-year-olds would not have H1 put on their record card. Thus the levels are only reminders to support the Attainment Target and need not be covered in detail. If a child has interest in history, he/she has knowledge and can use sources to tell him/her about the past. The main signs of this are reading, looking at pictures in books and on postcards, looking at buildings and talking about the past. All these signs may only show themselves spasmodically at this stage of schooling.

KEY STAGE 2

Advice about Key Stage 2 is necessarily more speculative than Key Stage 1. Therefore my suggestions may be open to more alteration than in the case of Key Stage 1. In order not to appear too test-conscious, teachers should build up spasmodic records unobtrusively, according to their school's record system, over the four years. This should be based on written work done on each of the eight units (kept in individual folders), discussion and response to visits. Although more knowledge will be needed and more emphasis placed on the Attainment Target, some of the Key Stage 1 tests could be used, especially for less able children, not reaching the present level 3 of the level descriptions. During the summer term of Year 6, when no work on a specific unit should be done, a final record should be made, taking into account the previous assessments in Years 3, 4 and 5. Each year record should be based on 'degrees of interest' as follows:

H1 = great interest
H2 = satisfactory interest
H3 = little interest

Thus the Year 6 final assessment represents all four years. The history coordinator should be involved with this final assessment to be handed over to the secondary school. If a child has missed one of the units, tests or visits, enough will have been done to reach one of the three 'degrees'.

Examples of work to test for the Attainment Target on the Anglo-Saxons (unit 1) might be an account of the life of King Alfred from birth to death providing evidence of sequencing for the Attainment Target. Two contemporary extracts from the Venerable Bede's *History* could be used as evidence of Britain's conversion to Christianity, so fulfilling the use of historical sources. The martyrdom of St Alban, a newly converted Christian, and the conversion of King Ethelbert of Kent by Augustine from Rome, tell children much of the emotion, enthusiasm and sacrifice of the Christians as well as the power of Christianity in the early centuries AD. These extracts are short, impelling and clear accounts, and understandable by most juniors. Work on Extension study A 'Domestic life, families and childhood' might take the form of the making of a time-line and pictures from 1500 to the present

day on how wash day was carried out in the intervening years using available materials (and perhaps evaluating these as evidence). This could also be done for schooling, clothing and food. These are only two examples, and more would be needed for the remaining units. Several suggestions have been made by publishers as to how Key Stages 1 and 2 history may be assessed and recorded. Until Sir Ron Dearing has listened to different points of view on this and decisions have been made, it is difficult to simplify these decisions for teachers. But assessment in history in Key Stages 1 and 2 should encourage children to be readers of history throughout life.

ELEVEN

The way ahead

The National Curriculum in History in the primary school is a good beginning as it stands, but there are pointers for the 'way ahead'. By the summer of 1993, only four out of the six primary years will have experienced it, therefore any assessment of its implementation would be more valid in 1995. Meanwhile some teachers and others are already systematically monitoring the introduction of National Curriculum Primary History.

More advantages than disadvantages have come to young children. More history is taught than under the 'topic' regime, there is more structure and less overlapping of content, and teachers and children are reading more. This particularly applies to Key Stage 1, though 'Life before 1900' tends to get neglected. The need to impart more historical knowledge has given impetus to whole-class teaching, more story-telling and greater use of a wider range of historical sources. Teachers are trying to link knowledge, skills and concepts more obviously. The new coordinators of humanities have meant more help for teachers and discussion about history. Government, local education authorities and subject associations are providing positive help in the form of in-service work. The booklets being published by the National Curriculum Council and Schools Examination and Assessment Council (and in future School Curriculum and Assessment Authority) are scholarly and good for reference, but schools and teachers need to use them selectively and apply them to their own situations. The booklet on non-European study units is particularly helpful for sources.

Secondary school history teachers should no longer 'begin at the beginning' and are assured that each child will have some assessment at age eleven. They know that the core British history study units have been attempted, therefore the Key Stage 3 units (2, 3 and 4) have been experienced. Above all, children have done more reading and writing of history and have become familiar with time-lines and discussion of sources. Thus the work of children when they embark on Key Stage 3, and therefore also the task of secondary teachers, has become easier, however well or badly juniors have been taught.

But the implementation of the National Curriculum in History has shown up weaknesses which need attention in 'the way ahead'. In the words of an article in *Education 3–13* 'the planned curriculum will change as it is implemented' and 'implementing will transform the curriculum by the mid-1990s' (Knight, Farmer and Hewitt, 1991). The most obvious problem is the weight of work for teachers in their preparation. It is to be hoped that the 1994 Dearing Proposals will alleviate this.

Another problem for some schools, particularly small ones, has been the provision of varied resources – for example, more than one series of 'textbooks'. Thirdly, teachers have had to teach units without adequate in-service provision and reading time for themselves. Lastly, assessment, now teacher-initiated, may still be a bogey with the danger that more time may be spent assessing children individually than in preparing and teaching the history to be assessed.

Before the Final Order was published in March 1991, many experienced educationists had warned of the need for future changes. As early as 1988, Tom Arkle wrote of the whole five-to-sixteen range in history, 'any national curriculum that does not encourage and permit further substantial development in the teaching of history should be regarded automatically as being unacceptable' (Arkle, 1988). In a paper written in 1989, the National Union of Teachers advised that the 'consultative process . . . should continue even beyond the establishment of the National Curriculum'. Indeed, the Final Report of History Working Group (April, 1990) itself foretold the need for 'flexibility, new ideas and revision' and it was 'to keep for some years then add and take away', and 'any new units may need more resources and training' (*Final Report*, 9.33 and 9.34, pp. 175–6). In an amazingly far-sighted

article (for 1991) Knight, Farmer and Hewitt earmarked five factors influencing change. They are: changed expectations of the meaning of history in school; the scope of selection of content in the present system; the need for teacher assessment to be 'confident' over the country; and the influence of 'tailor-made' books for the National Curriculum. They emphasised in particular that the issue of separate subject teaching or integrated teaching would be resolved in the following way. At first, history would be taught as a separate subject. Then there would be progression to history-centred topics supported by two other subjects. In other words integration, as embodied in the well-known topic approach will 're-emerge in a revised and strengthened form'. It remains to be seen how far schools will use the post-Dearing provisions to encourage – or discourage – that 're-emergence'.

THE 1994 DEARING PROPOSALS AND BEYOND

The slimming down of National Curriculum History through the 1994 Proposals has my wholehearted support. It will alleviate the load of teacher preparation, but results in contact time with children being cut to thirty-six hours per year at Key Stage 1, and forty-five at Key Stage 2, in order to allow for one day per week free from National Curriculum obligations. Therefore there may not be any increase in time for classroom contact in history. It is to be hoped that the 'free' day per week will occasionally be used for history, especially when field work is involved, as in Extension study D at Key Stage 2.

It is with great relief that I see history retained at Key Stage 1, where much exciting work has been enjoyed in the past two years. Many of us have long thought that myths and legends were too difficult for infants; it is suitable that they have now become part of the core unit on

Ancient Greece. I also fully endorse the lack of emphasis on twentieth-century history and the reiteration that 'the past beyond living memory' is equally important. People and events in British history should be the chief contents, as having more points of reference for young children in Britain.

Key Stage 2 now constitutes one Programme of Study, consisting of four 'core units' and four 'extension studies'. More latitude has been given in these 'extension studies' to allow teachers to choose their own topics, maintaining the popular and effective study of the locality but with fewer provisos. The new study in depth (Extension study D) as a 'patch' approach allows even more latitude, so much so that some teachers may need help with how to choose their study and how to find and use contemporary written sources. The packs of documents ('archive teaching units')

produced by Local Education Authorities and
Record Offices in the 1970s should be taken out
of the cupboard if they are still there, and dusted
down. The words 'an important historical issue'
can be misleading, as many buildings and writers
(e.g. Shakespeare) constitute very suitable depth
studies. According to the 1994 Proposals, the four
core units should have most time spent on them,
and the extension studies should explain and
develop these. The eight units are written so as to
enable slow-learning pupils to undertake parts of
them in order to reach at least Level 1. For this
purpose I am pleased to see 'Queen Victoria and
her family' specifically mentioned in core unit 3.
The main difficulty for slow learners is the lack of
suitable resources for history (see p. 100).

'The way ahead' is therefore promising for
history in the primary school. History is already
being taught more successfully than at any time in
the past. What is now needed is more experience
and detailed study of the more flexible policies
suggested by Dearing and of how these policies
are implemented in schools. It will be important
to examine the effectiveness of different
approaches to the learning and teaching of
primary history, and of the continuing influence
of published books and materials, both those
presently in use and those of the future. Dearing's
recommendations about the role of primary
history in the education of children with special
educational needs (SEN) will require particular
monitoring.

We now need to see the next phase of primary
history (1995–2000) carried out with the
unhurried professional authority and expertise
that was conspicuously lacking in the first dash for
the National Curriculum. This is where teachers,
researchers and administrators can and should
work together to ensure that history is retained as
a full and effective component in the education
of all young children.

Appendix 1 – Software

This material on software has been written by Grahame Banks of the Faculty of Education at the University of the West of England.

GENERAL

In many respects, some of the 'content-free' software, for example, databases and material designed for use with the concept keyboard, will provide the teacher with the most flexible learning resources. However, the time commitment required for the preparation of materials for use with this type of software may prove prohibitive for some teachers. Nevertheless, I have included some examples of this type of software.

Newsextra
A simulation of the flow of news into a newsroom. Cross-curricular. Used very successfully in our Aztec work with students and children.
Northwest Semerc, Fitton Hill CDC, Rosary Road, Oldham, OL8 2QE (061 627 4469).

Teletype
Newsroom simulation.
Sherston Software, Swan Barton, Sherston, Malmesbury, Wiltshire, SN16 0LH (0666 840433).

Time-lines
Create your own time-line with pictures and symbols.
Soft Teach Educational, Sturgess Farm, Longbridge Deverill, Warminster, Wiltshire, BA12 7EA (0985 40329).

Touch Explorer Plus
Concept keyboard required. This 'content-free' package allows children to explore an environment created by themselves or by the teacher. Information can be built up over a series of levels. It is particularly useful for exploring a picture of, say, a series of artefacts, a building or a simple plan or map. As with most good software, it is best used alongside other non-IT resources.
Resource, Exeter Road, Wheatley, Doncaster, South Yorkshire, DN2 4PY (0302 340331).

Typesetter
A very useful word processor that can produce headlines and boxes – good for news simulations.
Sherston Software, Swan Barton, Sherston Malmesbury, Wiltshire, SN16 0LH (0666 840433).

KEY STAGE 1

Castle Pack
Pack of materials including database of people living in a castle, plan of a castle and workcards.
Resource, Exeter Road, Wheatley, Doncaster, South Yorkshire, DN2 4PY (0302 340331).

Arcventure
A simulation of an archaeological dig. 'Finds' can be identified and 'reconstructed'.
Sherston Software, Swan Barton, Sherston Malmesbury, Wiltshire, SN16 0LH (0666 840433).

KEY STAGE 2

Core unit 1 – Romans, Anglo-Saxons and Vikings in Britain

Isca
Exploring life in Roman Britain through role-play. Utilises datafiles, maps and buildings.
ESM, Abbeygate House, East Road, Cambridge, CB1 1DB (0223 65445).

Core unit 2 – Life in Tudor times

Mary Rose
A simulation which allows children to 'discover' and explore the wreck of the *Mary Rose*.
Cambridge Software House, 7 Free Church Passage, St Ives, Huntingdon, Cambridgeshire (0480 67945).

Core unit 3 – Victorian Britain

The Victorians
Based on the real village of Wookey, Somerset. A simulation of life in a Victorian village.
BBC Software, 124 Cambridge Science Park, Milton Road, Cambridge, CB4 4ZS (0223 42558).

Core unit 5 – Ancient Greece

Ancient Greece
An exploration of some of the important sites of Ancient Greece.
Chalksoft, PO Box 49, Spalding, Lincolnshire, PE11 1NZ (0775 769518).

Extension unit C – The Aztecs

Explorations and encounters
Includes four computer programs, pupils' books and teachers' notes. Comes in two main parts – 'Search for the New World' and 'The Kingdom of Gold'.
Tressell Publications Ltd, Lower Ground Floor, 70 Grand Parade, Brighton, BN2 2JA (0273 600186).

Touch Explorer Plus
National Council for Educational Technology, Sir William Lloyds Road, Science Park, University of Warwick, Coventry, CN4 7EZ (0203 416944).

Appendix 2 – Asking questions about a building

Whatever the building (Roman fort, Norman church, Victorian station, modern airport) certain questions can be asked about it:

- When was it built?
- Why was it built?
- Why was this site chosen?
- Who built it?
- What materials have been used in its construction: for walls, roofing, floors, ceilings?
- Is the building still used for its original function?
- Is there evidence of repair, rebuilding or extension?
- Is the building still being used? If not, when was it last occupied? Why is it now vacant?

- Can you find evidence of this building in engravings, drawings, photographs?
- Can you find evidence of this building on historical maps?
- Can you find out how much the building cost when it was originally constructed?
- Can you find out anything about the building methods used in its construction (for example, tools and equipment) and the size of the labour force which was required to build it?

(From Henry Pluckrose *Children learning History*, Simon and Schuster, (1991))

Appendix 3 – Select resources for teachers and children

This list is highly selective and personal. It omits the more obvious resources and gives suggestions and a few examples, rather than detailed information. Some items, particularly those for Key Stage 1, could appear under several headings but are put under one. Only those suitable at the time of writing have been noted.

GUIDES TO THE NATIONAL CURRICULUM IN HISTORY

Longman ('A Sense of History') and Ginn ('Ginn History') have published materials for all units in Key Stages 1 and 2, including teachers' resource books, pictures and books for children to read. Ginn provides stories 'pre–1900' for Key Stage 1.

Cambridge Guide to Museums of Britain and Ireland. Hudson, K. and Nicholson, A. (1987) (Cambridge University Press).
History-based Topic Work. (1987) (Education Department, County Hall, Trowbridge, Wiltshire).
History Key Stage 1. Blueprints. Clemson, W. (1991) (Stanley Thornes).
Practical Guides: History. Hill, C. and Morris, J. (1991) (Scholastic Publications).

History Key Stage 2. Blueprints. Palmer, J. (1992) (Stanley Thornes).
Time and Place. History 1 and 2. For Key Stage 2. Harrison, P. and S. (1992) (Simon and Schuster).
Teachers' Resource Book and *Picture Resource Book* (Flopover). Hughes, P. (1993) (Oxford University Press). This series includes 'pre-1900' stories for Key Stage 1.
Museums and Art Galleries. (British Leisure Publishers) (annually).

These guides help teachers to work through the History National Curriculum but do not select or express authors' views.

ORGANISATIONS

Radio and television
Various companies provide programmes (for example, 'Landmarks', 'Zigzag', 'Time-lines', 'Watch', 'History', etc.), videos, packs and books for teachers and children. They have adapted very well to the National Curriculum and gained support from Pictorial Charts Educational Trust in providing contemporary pictures and wall charts.

BBC Educational Publishing, PO Box 234, Wetherby, West Yorkshire, LS23 7EU.

Channel 4, The Educational Television Company, PO Box 100, Warwick, CU34 6TZ.

Curriculum Council for Wales (CCW)
Materials to help Welsh and also English teachers. Castle Building, Womanby Street, Cardiff, CF1 9SX.

English Heritage
Buildings, *Remnants* magazine, packs (for example, Osborne House) and Teachers' Guides to portraits, listed buildings, school buildings, objects, houses, story-telling at historical sites (on tape). Also books such as *Ration Book Recipes 1939–54* and *Living History*. Also videos (for example, Bosobel House).
Keysign House, 429 Oxford Street, London, W1R 2HD.

Group for Education in Museums (Gem)
For conferences, newsletters and journals. Emma Webb, Museum of London, London Wall, London, EC27 5HN.

Historical Association
Primary membership – *Primary History* three times a year. Conferences twice a year. Pamphlets, for example, 'Bringing History to Life' series; 'Implementing the National Curriculum' (for example, the Romans); 'History through Drama'; 'Historical Fiction in the Classroom'. *Primary History Today*; Occasional Paper 2.
59a Kennington Park Road, London, SE11 4JH.

Mexicolore
Aztec replicas.
28 Warriner Gardens, London, SW11 4EB.

The National Trust
Buildings; National Trust Young Theatre; books for children to read (for example, *Crisis at Crabtree, Investigating Food in History, Investigating Family History, Scrub-a-dub Nellie, The House of Whispers*).
Education Office, 8 Church Street, Locock, Chippenham, Wiltshire, SN15 2LG.

Replicas
'Articles of Antiquity', Bury Business Centre, Kay Street, Bury, Lancashire, BL9 6BU.
'History in Evidence', Unit 4, Holmewood Field Business Park, Park Road, Holmewood, Chesterfield, S42 5UY.

SENS (Special Educational Needs Support Service) Radcliffe Street Centre, Royton, Oldham, OL2 6RH. (Materials on Vikings, Tudors and Stuarts.)

St Albans Cathedral Education Centre Booklets on St Alban (by Matthew Paris), *Abbey People* (suitable for Key Stage 1). Sumpter Yard, St Albans, AL1 1BY

Tumi (Latin American Craft Centre), 23/24 Chalk Farm Road, Camden Town, London NW1.

PUBLISHERS

Anglia Young Books. Very good on stories. Durhams Farmhouse, Butcher's Hill, Ickleton, Saffron Walden, Essex, CB10 1SR.

A & C Black. Very good hardback reading books for all ages five to eleven (for example, 'Turn of the Century' series and *Pot Luck* (food through the ages)).

Longman has provided history books for primary children for many years. The 'Then and There' series is particularly useful for teachers as background reading (for example *Shakespeare and his Theatre, The Elizabethan Country House, Children at Work*).

Pictorial Charts Educational Trust (PCET), 27 Kirchen Road, London, W13 0LD, has published many wall charts of contemporary pictures for most units of the National Curriculum (for example, *British History Timelines, Family Packs, Tudor and Stuart Timelines* (to accompany Channel 4 series) and *Stories from the Past* (for Key Stage 1)).

Scholastic Publications. *Infant Projects* (bi-monthly magazine), *Junior Focus, Child* and *Junior Education* (monthly) – *Victorian Britain*, a pack of six posters. Many packs for Key Stages 1 and 2 National Curriculum (e.g. *The Tudors*).

Tressell Publications has published very useful books on primary sources (for example, *The Great Fire of London* and *The Plague of London*) and also a good integrated project for Key Stage 1 – *Ourselves*. Lower Ground Floor, 70 Grand Parade, Brighton, BN2 2JA.

Wayland do not publish a National Curriculum series but specialise in reading books for children aged five to eleven (for example, *The Greeks, The Saxons, Saxon Invaders and Settlers, The Gunpowder Plot, Tudor Towns*).

SPECIFIC BOOKS FOR NATIONAL CURRICULUM UNITS

Many units are omitted as being well supplied. Books helpful to teachers for the content of history include:

A Children's History of Britain and Ireland. Wright, C. (1993) (Kingfisher).
Boys and Girls of History and *More Boys and Girls of History.* Power, E. and R. (1977) (Dennis Dobson).

Books for children to read include:

Key Stage 1
'Starting History' packs (Scholastic Publications).
'Changing Times' series (Franklin Watts).
'My Book About', for example, *Houses and Homes* and *Toys* (Wayland).
'Starting History', for example, *Our Holidays* and *What We Wore* (Wayland).
A Victorian Sunday. Faulkner, S. and L. (1993) (Wayland).
Sir Francis Drake – His Daring Deeds. Gerrard, R. (1992) (Gollanz).

Unit 2 – Life in Tudor Times
The Boy Who Sailed with Columbus. Foreman, M. (Pavilion).

Unit 3 – Victorian Britain
The Victorian Schoolday. Frankum, W. and Lawrie, J. (Education Library Service, Shire Hall, Shinfield Park, Reading, Berkshire, RG2 9XD).

Unit 4 – Britain since 1930
Emma's War – Three books on World War II (Egon).

Extension study A
Houses and Homes (link with technology). Hamilton Maclaren, A. (1991) (Wayland).
The Farmer Through History. Chrisp, P. (1993) (Wayland).
Murray and Simon and Schuster are to publish more books (for example, *Ships and Seafarers* (Simon and Schuster)). HarperCollins have published packs.

Extension study B (local history)
My History Scrapbook. Montford, S. (1993) (Wayland).
Look Around-Outside. Pluckrose, H. (1986) (Heinemann).

Extension study C (Non-European)
Pharaoh's Flowers. Hepper, F. N. (1990) (HMSO).

MUSIC

A Musical Calendar of Festivals (1983) (Ward Lock).

Music from the Past (1986 [Victorian], 1987 [Tudor and Stuart], 1988 [Medieval]) (books, tapes and pamphlets of Tudor, Stuart and Victorian times). Bagenal, A. and M. (Longman).

Music and Family Life (1993) (books and tapes of Tudor, Stuart and Georgian times). Bagenal, A. and M. (Oxford University Press).

The Singing Game. Opie, I. and P. (1985) (Oxford University Press).

Tapes of music to accompany *A Sense of History.* Purkis, S. (ed.) (1992) (Longman).

Tinderbox (1982) (A & C Black).

Singing Games for Children (1990) Telstar Video Entertainment Ltd, The Studio, 5 King Edward Mews, Byfield Gardens, Barnes, London, SW13 9HP.

Over the Rainbow (multicultural children's rhymes) Third Eye Centre/SCRC, Glasgow – also from Letterbox Library, Unit 2D, Leroy House, 436 Essex Road, London, N1 3QP.

For musical instruments for children to make and play, apply to A. and M. Bagenal, 45 West Street, Godmanchester, Huntingdon, Cambridgeshire, PE18 8HA.

For cassettes such as *Music of the Tudor Age, Shakespeare Songs, Tudor Christmas Music,* apply to: Past Times, Witney, Oxfordshire, OX8 6BH or any other Past Times shop.

MUSEUMS

Museums have adapted very well to the National Curriculum. They provide in-service courses and booklets to help teachers with children's visits. A few examples of such museums are:

City of Bristol Museum and Art Gallery – provides booklet *Children in Pictures* (Queen's Road, Bristol, BS8 1RL).

British Museum – excellent for help with 'ancient civilisations' (Education Service, Great Russell Street, London, WC1 3DG).

National Maritime Museum – helpful with, for example, Armada publications (1988) (Romney Road, Greenwich, London, SE10 9NF).

National Portrait gallery – provides packs of Tudor and Stuart postcards and posters (St Martin's Place, London, WC2H 0HE).

The Walker Art Gallery – provides pamphlets and postcards of Greek myths and Tudor portraits (William Brown Street, Liverpool, L3 8EL).

ORAL HISTORY

Books which might help here include:

An Introductory Guide to Oral History in the National Curriculum. Redfern, A. (1993) (Oral History Society, c/o Department of Sociology, Essex University, Wivenhoe Park, Colchester, CO4 3SQ).

Oral History, National Curriculum. Spring 1992, Vol. 20 No. 1 (Journal of the Oral History Society).

Oral History – Talking about the Past. Perks, R. (1992) (Historical Association).

Back to Your Roots. (1993) BBC pamphlet.

Age Concern and Help the Aged are also concerned with oral history.

References

Chapter 1

MARWICK, A. (1970) *The Nature of History* (p. 13). Macmillan.

COLLINGWOOD, R. G. (1946) *The Idea of History* (p. 10). Oxford University Press.

SLATER, J. (1978) 'Why History?', *Trends*, Spring (p. 5).

BLYTH, J. E. (1981) 'Helping Young Children to Understand the Past', *Early Childhood Education*, November (p. 5).

Chapter 2

CARR, E. H. (1961) *What is History?* (p. 7). Macmillan.

FONTANA, D. (ed.) (1984) *The Education of the Young Child* (p. 5). Blackwell (now Simon and Schuster).

MINISTRY OF EDUCATION (1952) *Teaching History*. No. 23. HMSO.

BRYANT, P. (1974) *Perception and Understanding in Young Children*. Methuen.

DONALDSON, M. (1978) *Children's Minds*. Fontana.

Chapter 3

KNIGHT, P. (1989) 'Research on Teaching and Learning in History – A perspective from Afar', *Social Education*, September (p. 308).

KNIGHT, P. (1992) 'Myth and Legend at Key Stage 1 – The case of Robin Hood', *Primary Teaching Studies*, Vol. 6, No. 3, pp. 237–44.

KNIGHT, P. (1989) 'A study of teaching and children's understanding of people in the past', *Research in Education*, No. 44, pp. 39–53.

COOPER, H. (1992) *The Teaching of History* (Studies in Primary Education). David Fulton Publishers.

LYNN, S. (1993) 'Children Reading Pictures: History Visuals at Key Stages 1 and 2', *Education 3–13*, Vol. 21, No. 3, pp. 23–9. *see also* HARNETT, P. (1993) 'Identifying Progression in Children's Understanding: the use of visual materials to assess primary school children's learning of History', *Cambridge Journal of Education*, Vol. 23, No. 2, pp. 137–53.

SWIFT, R. and JACKSON, M. (1987) *Primary Schools: a Regional Survey*. Chester College, Cheyney Road, Chester, CH1 4BJ.

DEPARTMENT OF EDUCATION AND SCIENCE (DES) (1989) *The Teaching and Learning of History and Geography* (Aspects of Primary Education). HMSO.

PLUCKROSE, H. (1991) *Children Learning History*. Blackwell (now Simon and Schuster).

BLYTH, J. (1989/1990) *History in Primary Schools*. Open University Press.

BLYTH, J. (1988) *History 5 to 9*. Hodder and Stoughton.

HILL, C. and MORRIS, J. (1991) *Practical Guides: History*. Scholastic Publications.

KNIGHT, P. (1991) *History in Key Stages 1 and 2*. Longman.

WRIGHT, M. (1992) *The Really Practical Guide to Primary History*. Stanley Thornes.

Nuffield Primary History Project – contact Mrs Jennie Vass, NPHP, School of Education, University of Exeter, Heavitree Road, Exeter, EX1 2JU.

Chapter 4

BOOTH, M. (1993) 'Studies in Historical Thinking and the National Curriculum in England', *Theory and Research in Education*, Winter, Vol. XXI, No. 1.

FINES, J. and HOPKINS, T. (1992) *Teaching for Attainment Target 2 in National Curriculum History*. Occasional Paper 5, Historical Association.

KNIGHT, P. (1991) *History in Key Stages 1 and 2* (p. 32). Longman.

Chapter 6

WOOD, M. (1981) *In Search of the Dark Ages*. BBC.

BEDE, (1990) *Ecclesiastical History of the English People*. Penguin Classics.

LAWRIE, J. and NOBLE, P. (1990) *Victorian Times*. Unwin Hyman (now HarperCollins).

JOHN MURRAY. (1912) *Queen Victoria's Diaries 1832–40*.

TAYLOR, A. J. P. (1965) *English History 1914–1945* (p. 302). Oxford University Press.

FOREMAN, M. (1989) *War Boy*. Pavilion Books.

HUGHES, P. and COX, K. (1992) *History: Timesavers*. Scholastic Publications.

HILL, C. and MORRIS, J. (1991) *Practical Guides: History*. Scholastic Publications.

WORSNOP, R. (1991) *Ancient Greece*. Collins.

HUGHES, P. and TWEEDIE, P. (1993) *Historical Maps*. Scholastic Publications.

LAVENDER, R. (1975) *Myths, Legends and Lore*. Blackwell (now Simon and Schuster).

MASON, J. (1991) *Greek Heroes and Monsters*. A Sense of History. Longman.

LINES, K. (1973; paperback, 1986) *The Faber Book of Greek Legends*. Faber.

Stories of the Past. H 713 (1993) Pictorial Charts Educational Trust.

HORTON, A. M. (1992) *Teaching About Aztecs: A Cross-Curricular Perspective*. 'Bringing History to Life' series P4. Historical Association.

TRESSELL PUBLICATIONS. (1991) *Explorations and Encounters*. (Four computer programs, pupils' book and teachers' notes.) Tressell Publications Ltd.

TOUCH EXPLORER PLUS (software). Resource Software, Exeter Road, Wheatley, Doncaster, South Yorkshire, DN2 4PY.

Chapter 7

JEFFREYS, M. V. C. (1939) *History in Schools: the Study of Development*. Pitman.

HILL, C. and MORRIS, J. (1991) *Practical Guides: History*. Scholastic Publications.

TEACHING HISTORY RESEARCH GROUP (1991) *History in the National Curriculum*. Heinemann.

HUGHES, P. and COX, K. (1991) *Starting History – Homes*. Scholastic Publications.

PURKIS, S. (1981) *At home in 1900*. Longman.

REEVES, M. (1980) *Why History?* Longman.

SWIFT, R. and DUNN, D. (1991) *Houses Through the Ages*. Local History in the National Curriculum. Chester College History Department, Cheyney Road, Chester, CH1 4BJ.

DEPARTMENT FOR SCIENCE AND EDUCATION (DES) (1989) 'Good Practice Observed' in *The Teaching and Learning of History and Geography*. (Aspects of Primary Education). HMSO.

PINNELL (1986) *Village Heritage*. Alan Sutton.

WAPLINGTON, A. (ed.) (1986) *History Around You* (series for children to read). Oliver and Boyd.

ROGERS, A. (1972) *This Was Their World* (p. xii). Approaches to Local History. BBC.

BLYTH, J. (1990) *History in Primary Schools*. Open University Press.

see also PURKIS, S. (1993) 'Support for the Supplementaries', *Primary History*, No. 4, June, Historical Association.

Chapter 8

ALEXANDER, R., ROSE, T. and WOODHEAD, C. (1992) 'Three Wise Men' in *Curriculum Organisation and Classroom Practice in the Primary School: a Discussion Paper*. DES.

THOMAS, N. (1992) 'That Discussion Paper', *Education 3–13*, Vol. 20, No. 3, October.

CAMPBELL, R. J. (1990) Editorial, *Education 3–13*. Vol. 18.

DEPARTMENT OF EDUCATION AND SCIENCE (DES) (1989) *The Teaching and Learning of History and Geography* (Aspects of Primary Education). HMSO.

NATIONAL CURRICULUM COUNCIL (NCC) (1993) *The National Curriculum in Keys Stages 1 and 2*. NCC.

COOPER, H. (1992). *The Teaching of History*. (Studies in Primary Education). David Fulton.

DEPARTMENT OF EDUCATION AND SCIENCE (DES) (1985) *Better Schools*. HMSO.

NOBLE, P. (1986) *Understanding History* (for W. H. Smith). Hodder and Stoughton.

NICHOL, J. (1981) *What is History?* Evidence in History. Blackwell (now Simon and Schuster).

HARRISON, M. (ed.) (1993) *Beyond the Core Curriculum*. Northcote House.

CAMPBELL, R. J. (1985) *Developing the Primary School Curriculum*. Holt.

see also WEBB, R. (1993) *Eating the Elephant Bit by Bit*. Association of Teachers and Lecturers.

see also BAGE, G. (1993) 'History at KS 1 and KS 2: questions of teaching, planning, assessment and progression', *The Curriculum Journal*, Vol. 4, No. 2, Summer.

Chapter 9

MARRIOTT, S. (1992) 'Pictures and Nursery Rhymes', *Education 3–13*, Vol. 20, No. 3, October.

MORRIS, S. (1989) *A Teacher's Guide to Using Pictures*. English Heritage.

HOSKINS, W. G. (1976) *The Age of Plunder*. Longman.

MACAULAY, D. (1975) *Pyramid*. Collins.

BAGENAL, A. and M. (1986, 1987 and 1988) *Music from the Past*. (series). Longman.

OPIE, I. and P. (1985) *The Singing Game*. Oxford University Press.

KNIGHT, P. and GREEN, A. (1993) 'History Schemes KS 2' in *Education 3–13*, Vol. 21, No. 3.

TAYLOR, A. (1993) 'Period piece' in *The Times Educational Supplement*, (A visit to Sevington School) 15 October 1993.

Chapter 10

BLYTH, J. (1990) *History in Primary Schools* (pp. 65–70). Open University Press.

COLWELL, E. (1991) *Storytelling*. Thimble Press.

HUGHES, P. and COX, K. (1991) *Starting History – Homes*. Scholastic Publications.

SCHOOLS EXAMINATION AND ASSESSMENT COUNCIL (1993) *Children's Work Assessed – Geography and History*. HMSO.

Chapter 11

KNIGHT, P., FARMER, A. and HEWITT, J. (1991) 'Implementation and Change in the Primary Curriculum. History in the 1990s', *Education 3–13*. Vol. 19, No. 2, June.

ARKLE, T. (1988) 'History's role in the School Curriculum', *Journal of Education Policy*, Vol. 3, No. 1.

NATIONAL UNION OF TEACHERS (NUT) (1989) *Discussion Paper on the History National Curriculum* (before the Interim Report).

HISTORY WORKING GROUP (April 1990) *Final Report*. HMSO.

Texts relating to the teaching of history – Key Stages 1 and 2 (mainly published since 1988)

Key Stage 1

COOPER, H. (1994) *History in the First Three Years of School* (*Teaching and Learning in the First Three Years of School*). Routledge.

HUGHES, P. and COX, K. (1990) *Early Years' History: An Approach Through Story*. Liverpool Institute of Higher Education.

In Touch with the Past. (1983) Resources for Learning Development Unit Bristol.

PALMER, J. and PETTIT, D. (1993) 'History and topic work' in *Topic Work in the Early Years*. Routledge.

SNELGROVE, L. E. (1986) *Storyline History* (four volumes). Oliver and Boyd.

TEACHING HISTORY RESEARCH GROUP (1991) *History in the National Curriculum*. Heinemann.

Under Fives and Museums (1989). Ironbridge Gorge Museum.

WEST, J. and M. (1991) *Magic Map*. The Infant Telltale. Elm Publications.

Key Stages 1 and 2

ANDREETTI, K. (1992) *Teaching History from Primary Evidence* (the Roehampton Teaching Studies series). David Fulton.

BLYTH, J. (1990) *History in Primary Schools*. Open University Press.

COOPER, H. (1992) *The Teaching of History*. Studies in Primary Education. David Fulton.

DEPARTMENT OF EDUCATION AND SCIENCE (DES) (1989) *The Teaching and Learning of History and Geography* (Aspects of Primary Education). HMSO.

EVANS, H. and M. (1986) *Picture Researchers' Handbook*. Van Nostrand.

KNIGHT, P. (1991) *History in Key Stages 1 and 2*. Longman.

KNIGHT, P. (1993) *Primary Geography: Primary History*. David Fulton.

PLUCKROSE, H. (1991) *Children Learning History*. Blackwell (now Simon and Schuster).

PUMFREY, P. and VERMA, G. (eds) (1994) *Cultural Diversity and the Curriculum*, Vol. 3, *Foundation Subjects and R.E.* The Falmer Press.

REEVES, M. (1980) *Why History?* Longman.

Teaching History at Key Stage 2. (1994) National Curriculum Council.

WILLIG, J. (1990) *Children's Concepts and the Primary Curriculum*. Paul Chapman.

WRIGHT, M. (1992) *Primary History* (The Really Practical Guide series). Stanley Thornes.

Index